Contents

Week 1: Preparing for a Hope Infusion

Overflowing Hope! . . . 2
4 Questions that Determine My Hope Level . . . 3
Replace Anxiety with Hope . . . 4
An Anchor in the Storm . . . 5
Hope in God's Word . . . 6
Hope is an Antidote to Fear . . . 7
Hope Gives Wings . . . 8
Small Group Lesson 1: Hope Floats Your Boat . . . 9

Week 2: The Foundation of Hope

My View of God . . . 20
Hope in Who? . . . 21
Hope Not in Hercules . . . 22
Two Things That Bring Hope! . . . 23
Hope in God, Not in Myths . . . 24
Hope in the Source, Not the Resource . . . 25
Hope in What's Certain . . . 26
Small Group Lesson 2: My View of God . . . 27

Week 3: The Most Common Thief of Hope

How Do I See Myself? . . . 34
Who Am I? . . . 35
Christ in Me, the Hope of Glory . . . 36
Hope After a Fall . . . 37
When God Makes a Valley into a Door . . . 38
Envy vs. Hope . . . 39
Once without Hope . . . 40
Small Group Lesson 3: The Most Common Thief of Hope . . . 41

Week 4: Spread Hope!

Spreading Hope. 50

Agents of Hope 51

Building Hope in Others with My Words 52

Share Reasons for Your Hope 53

The Effect of Hope 54

Hold on to Hope 55

My Hope Pleases God 56

Small Group Lesson 4: Building Hope in Others 57

Week 5: Living with Hope Daily

Expecting the Best 64

Living with Daily Expectation 65

The Suspense is Part of the Fun 66

Joyful in Hope 67

Beyond Pessimism and Optimism 68

Living Hope that Never Fades 69

Hope in the Midst of Trouble. 70

Small Group Lesson 5: Am I a Yesterday Person or a Tomorrow Person? . . . 71

Week 6: Hope when Life Seems Hopeless

When Hope is Shattered 76

When God Seems Silent. 77

Hope in the Dark 78

Prisoners of Hope. 79

Wait until the End of the Story. 80

Motivated by Hope. 81

Hope When I Am Attacked 82

Small Group Lesson 6: Finding Hope When My Hope is Shattered. 83

Week 7: Our Ultimate Hope!

My Ultimate Hope 90
Get Ready, Boys! 91
More than a Metaphor. 92
Future Certain Hope 93
Endurance Inspired by Hope 94
Does Hope Make a Difference? 95
Hope Review. 96
Celebrate Hope!. 98
Small Group Lesson 7: The Ultimate Hope 99

Small Group Resources

Small Group Guidelines and Agreement 104
Small Group Values. 106
Guidelines for a Great Group. 107
Small Group Roster. 108
Small Group Prayer Requests 109
Questions Asked Frequently by Hosts 110
20 Ideas for Spreading Hope 111

Hope Resources

Songs About Hope 112
For Further Study 114
Meet the Authors. 115

Read This If You Want to Survive!

Hope is absolutely vital to your survival.

The book *The Survivor's Club* is written by a graduate of the Air Force Survival, Evasion, Resistance and Escape (SERE) training school. It has instructions on how to survive absolutely anything, from a plane crash to a sudden snowstorm to a mountain lion attack.

The author, Ben Sherwood, explains the Air Force "rule of threes" when stranded in an inhospitable environment:

> "You can survive 3 weeks without food; 3 days without water; 3 minutes without air... *but not three seconds without hope.*"

Hope. It's the confident assurance that I have a future; that better things are ahead; that today and tomorrow will bring new opportunities and rewards; that I have a destiny; that my efforts will bear fruit.

Yet a sense of hope in our personal and national future is being drained away.

As I write, CNBC is airing a special report calling this "an unparalleled age of uncertainty." Every year, 23 million Americans suffer from anxiety disorders — largely expressed in fear about their present and future — and that number is swelling. Even Christians are feeling hopeless: 62 percent of evangelical Christians now say they are worried about the future.

You might relate: Do you feel undeserving of a good future? Do you worry frequently about what's ahead? Even when things go well, are you secretly convinced it will all go horribly wrong?

Why are so many of us feeling such a lack of hope?

I think the answer is simple: The promises of God about our hope are no longer understood or believed — or even known! — by Christians today. As pastor and author John MacArthur says, "**Of the three supreme virtues — faith, hope, and love — hope is the most neglected.** The volumes written about faith and love would fill a small library, but studies on hope are surprisingly rare."

That's why we want to give you a **50-day hope experience.** We intend this daily devotional (and the accompanying small group video discussion guides and sermon series, found at www.HopeExperience.com) to **infuse you with hope each day.**

Hope for the Christian is more than mere optimism; it's grounded in the promises of God revealed in the Bible. So get to know those promises over the next 50 days and your life will be changed forever!

Here's the plan: Every day you'll read a short Bible passage about hope, ponder inspirational comments about hope, pray hopeful prayers, and engage in projects designed to bring hope to others.

I really believe you will find your optimism soaring, your perseverance strengthening, your joy increasing, and your character deepening as you immerse yourself in hope.

One note: Doing this experience with others will dramatically increase its effects as you encourage each other with words of hope. Gather friends and family if you can, get into a small group, check out the website, and dive in!

WEEK 1

PREPARING FOR A HOPE INFUSION

May the God of hope fill you with all joy and peace as you trust in him, so that you may overflow with hope by the power of the Holy Spirit! *[Romans 15:13]*

DAY

1

SUNDAY

by René Schlaepfer

What tends to overflow from my heart: Pessimism and worry, or optimism and hope? How is this reflected in my attitude?

PRAYER

Lord, instead of overflowing with anxiety, insecurity, or fear, help me to have so much hope inside me that I overflow with it.

Overflowing Hope!

> May the God of hope fill you with all joy and peace as you trust in him, so that you may overflow with hope by the power of the Holy Spirit. *[Romans 15:13]*

I love that phrase from today's verse: **"Overflow with hope"!**

I'll never forget seeing the Harlem Globetrotters basketball team at the Oakland Arena as a kid. During the game, star player and prankster Meadowlark Lemon doused a ref with a pail of water, then grabbed a second pail and ran through the aisles with it, threatening to pour it over the crowd. We all screamed as he ran right to the end of our row and then dumped the entire contents of the bucket over us... which to our surprise and delight contained only confetti!

I tell that story to point out a simple truth: **You can only overflow with what's been poured into you.** It's pointless to try to overflow with hope if you're busy pouring anxiety and fear into your life. Is your day filled with news reports about the latest disaster? Is your conversation full of gossip and criticism? Is your bedtime reading a source of stress? Then you'll overflow not with the clear water of hope, but with the confusing confetti of dread, pessimism, and negativity.

For at least the next seven weeks, try something else. **Try filling your mind with hope.**

Every day, for the next 50 days, read one of these devotions. Try to memorize the Scriptures, pray the prayers and consider the questions. Look for creative ways to spread hope through words and actions. And cut back as much as you can on any negative input (especially first thing in the morning, when you set the tone for the day, and last thing at night, when you essentially tell your mind how to dream).

You'll find in a few short weeks that you'll have a sense of relaxed optimism and a calm confidence — in short, you will overflow with hope!

In contrast to a freaked-out world, let's be people of joyful hope!

4 Questions that Determine My Hope Level

DAY
2
MONDAY
by René Schlaepfer

Be strong and take heart, all you who hope in the Lord.
[Psalm 31:24]

Read Psalm 31

As I share in the small group videos at www.HopeExperience.com, when I was young my father died of cancer. I remember reasoning, "I will protect myself from being hurt again by always imagining the worst possible outcome in life. That way I'll never be surprised when things go wrong!"

And so I did. The result of so much negative thinking was, of course, negative. As I grew, I became increasingly filled with insecurity, because that's what I had been pouring into my life!

This all began to change after a major adult anxiety attack landed me in the hospital. To counter my anxiety I put verses about the positive promises of God onto 3 x 5 cards and read them several times every day. Many of those verses are in this daily devotional! I noticed that each verse fell into one of four categories. In my observation, most people tend to lose hope when they have unbiblical answers to any of these four questions:

What is my view of God? Do I see Him as my loving Father, as my Good Shepherd, or is he a capricious and hard-to-please deity?

What is my view of myself? Am I a loser who tries and fails to do what is right, or am I chosen by God to be holy and blameless in His sight?

What will the future bring? Am I only going to be disappointed repeatedly, or am I destined for greatness, promised a bright future in heaven and opportunities on earth?

What is the outcome of suffering? Is it absurd and arbitrary, or does God promise never to waste a single tear that falls?

For years, my own answers to those questions were unbiblical — or at least incomplete — and so I was severely hope-deficient. But much like the shift in thinking at verse 14 of Psalm 31, my self-talk shifted from pity and pessimism to hopeful expectation. In this study, we'll look at the unshakable promises of God related to each question! Be strong and take heart, and prepare for a hope infusion!

What are my honest responses to the four questions in today's reading?

PRAYER

Lord, help me grow in hope during the next seven weeks!

DAY
3
TUESDAY
by René Schlaepfer

Replace Anxiety with Hope

> FOR EVERYTHING THAT WAS WRITTEN IN THE PAST WAS WRITTEN TO TEACH US, SO THAT THROUGH ENDURANCE AND THE ENCOURAGEMENT OF THE SCRIPTURES WE MIGHT HAVE HOPE.
> *[Romans 15:4]*

Read Romans 15:1–7

There's a lot of bad news in the world today. Anytime there's a disaster anywhere on the planet, the media announce it instantly. You can't get away from it: A plane has gone down, hostages have been taken, a gunman has gone berserk, an earthquake has occurred, poisonous gas has spilled. The availability of bad news is stunning, and it's not just limited to matters of international importance. I will never forget watching TV and hearing a serious announcer intone over dramatic music via a multi-million-dollar satellite uplink: "CNN Breaking News… The marriage of Jennifer Aniston and Brad Pitt is over!"

Thanks to technology we receive so much more input than people did just 20 years ago, and this is probably why there's a level of fear and anxiety in our society also unprecedented in history. In the past, only God was able to know as much bad news as we get every day, and I think still only God can really handle it!

As an antidote, bathe your mind in the Scriptures. In today's passage, Paul says that **everything that was written in the past was written so that we might have hope**.

Everything? Really? How can every story about Moses or Job or Sarah or David or Samson give you hope, filled as they are with strange mistakes and sins and conflicts? Well, for one thing, they were all flawed people, people who made mistakes and had doubts and argued with God. Yet He used them because He is full of grace and love. That means there's a future and a plan for you and me, too!

How do I allow God to encourage me with hope through the Scriptures every day? Do I spend too much time reading or watching things that drain my hope? Do I look to Scriptures specifically to give me hope, or are they more of an academic exercise for me?

PRAYER

Lord, thank You for giving me Scripture not just as a set of rules or as theological history, but in order that I might have hope!

ACTION

Another great antidote to negative media is positive media! For example, soak your mind with hope-filled music. A list of suggestions is on pages 112 and 113.

An Anchor in the Storm

DAY
4
WEDNESDAY
by René Schlaepfer

We have this hope as an anchor for the soul, firm and secure. *[Hebrews 6:19a]*

Read Hebrews 6:18–20

There's a nautical term used in the sailing world: "kedging." A kedge anchor is used when a ship is grounded or in rough seas. Sailors in a small boat will row the kedge anchor as far as they can from the ship in the general direction they want to move toward. They drop the kedge anchor into the sea. Then, back on board the ship, the sailors start the ship's winch and pull their way toward the anchor. That's "kedging."

We don't normally think of moving *toward* an anchor. An anchor usually represents the *past*. It holds us back. Sometimes, however, the anchor is our future. We move toward it. In turbulent times, or when we've run aground, we need to **pull ourselves into the future with the anchor of hope.**

The early Christians were anchored in this hope: Jesus not only died on the cross so that He forgives and hears us *now*; Jesus was resurrected, and that means one day in the *future* He will resurrect us too, to live in restored, immortal bodies. In fact the whole earth will be remade to show the glory it was meant to have from the beginning, and we'll live there together under God's peaceful reign. In the meantime, we are to act in the same way we'll act on the new heaven and new earth, as ambassadors of that future world.

It's been said the resurrection provides the "missing link" to our faith: Sure, we can catch glimpses of God's power while we live, but on a lot of days life can still feel futile. The resurrection erases the futility, and fills us with hope.

Winch yourself toward that anchor!

How does the promise of a resurrection serve as an anchor pulling me toward the future? How can this improve my outlook on life?

PRAYER

Lord, thank You for the assurance of the resurrection!

DAY

5

THURSDAY

by Robin Spurlock

Hope in God's Word

MAY THOSE WHO FEAR YOU REJOICE WHEN THEY SEE ME,
FOR I HAVE PUT MY HOPE IN YOUR WORD. *[Psalm 119:74]*

✹ ***Read Psalm 119:49–50***

I remember a time my daughter asked me to play a game with her. I was washing dishes and I told her I would play with her as soon as I finished. She left, set the game up and waited patiently for me to come. When I finished the dishes I moved on to something else forgetting my promise.

Pretty soon I was calling for her to get ready for bed and she came out of her room in tears. "But Mommy, you promised you would play a game with me. I have been waiting for you and you never came." I felt horrible! Too often we put our hope in another's word and the result is disappointment.

Psalm 119:74 reads *"...for I have put my hope in your word."* We can find ourselves wondering: Can I trust God and put my hope in His Word? Will He keep His promises? Sometimes it is hard to put my hope in His word in light of my experience with others. **But I can hope in His word because of who God is.** He is the Truth *[John 14:6]* and He cannot lie *[Hebrews 6:18]*. He is trustworthy!

In his book *Ruthless Trust,* Brennan Manning says, "Hope is the reliance on the promise of Jesus, accompanied by the expectation of fulfillment." For most of my life I had hoped with expectation in 2 Peter 3:9 as my family and I prayed for my father's salvation (nearly 50 years for my mom!). I knew God loved my dad, so I prayed for him daily, never giving up. Just a few hours before my dad's death, he surrendered his heart to the Lord. What joy! My hope in God's word was fulfilled even though it required me to wait and be patient. My faith was strengthened through the years by this test of endurance, especially during my dad's last days. As I trusted in God's word, my faith in Him increased. Even if I had never witnessed my father's first steps of faith, my own faith still would have grown over those years as I exercised my "hope muscle." In this 50-day study, you'll exercise that hope muscle, too!

Hope in God's Word. **It <u>never</u> fails!**

Do I ever let my past experiences with people who have disappointed me affect my hope in God? How will trusting in God's Word give me hope for what's ahead?

PRAYER

Lord, thank You for Your true, unfailing Word. Please give me the discipline to learn and memorize it and the faith to trust it.

Hope is an Antidote to Fear

DAY
6
FRIDAY
by Charlie Broxton

> "For I know the plans I have for you," declares the Lord, "plans to prosper you and not to harm you, plans to give you hope and a future." *[Jeremiah 29:11]*

✹ ***Read Jeremiah 29:10–14***

In his book *It's Not About the Bike*, renowned cyclist Lance Armstrong writes these words about hope: "Hope is the only antidote to fear." Whether he realized it or not, Armstrong stated a biblical truth.

So many of us spend a lot of our time listening to our fears and worries about the future. We do have a lot we could worry about — our family members, our future plans, our relationships, our dreams, our struggles, our financial situations, our needs — the list is endless. There's a true story about a time Stonewall Jackson had planned a daring attack. One of his generals fearfully objected saying, "I am afraid of this," and, "I worry that...." Jackson's answer to his general is still great advice for us today. He put his hand on his worrisome general's shoulder and said, **"General, never take counsel of your fears."**

In what area of my life am I taking counsel of my fears? What am I worried about right now? Have I brought it to God in prayer — and left it there?

For most of us, there are usually deeper questions behind our fears and worries: Does God have my best interest at heart? Can I trust God to take care of me? Is God truly good?

Jeremiah 29:11 answers this question emphatically: "*'For I know the plans I have for you,' declares the Lord, 'plans to prosper you and not to harm you, plans to give you hope and a future.'*"

This passage is all about hope. Hope in God's promise to take care of his people. Hope in God's plans for His people — in this life and the next. Hope in God's heart of love for His people. This passage teaches us that God does have our best interest at heart, He can be trusted to take care of us and He is good.

Next time you're tempted to take counsel of your fears, open your Bible and read Jeremiah 29:11. Read it until God's words of hope for you drown out the words of fear and worry. Read it until it becomes part of your heart. Read it until you are confident of God's good plans for your future — in this life and the next.

PRAYER

Thank You, God, for the plans You have for me; plans for hope and a future!

DAY

7

SATURDAY

by René Schlaepfer

Hope Gives Wings

✸ *Read Isaiah 40:21–31*

One of the greatest comeback stories in sports: San Francisco Giants pitcher Dave Dravecky's return from cancer. When a tumor was found in Dave's pitching arm, we fans thought his baseball days were over. Well, we were all wrong. I still get chills when I remember August 10, 1989, the day I tuned in to watch Dave defeat the Reds in his first major league game in over a year. He received twelve standing ovations, even from Reds fans!

But in his next start, his pitching arm snapped as he threw in the fifth inning. Doctors later discovered more cancer, and this time the whole arm had to be amputated.

Everyone wondered: How would Dave respond to this setback? He says he looked in the mirror following the surgery and prayed, "Okay, God. This is what I've got to live with. Put this behind me; let's go forward." As he walked the hospital corridor soon afterward, he came to a lounge where a whole family sat waiting during a surgery. The worried wife told him her husband had cancer. Dave sat down with them, and her son asked, "Where do you get your peace?" The entire family listened as he gently shared his faith. "It is hard to understand suffering in this life," he told them. "But you know, sooner or later *everything* on this earth is going to end. I believe God can and does heal people, but more important than that, I believe in the eternal hope of heaven. When I die, that's where I'm going. Heaven is my home." The conversation changed that family, and was the start of an international ministry to cancer patients.

Dave's strength and endurance is a testimony to the effect of biblical hope. Like today's scripture says, even the most impressive people are like dandelion seeds in a breeze compared to the permanence of God. But the good news is, I can find my permanent hope in Him:

> Those who hope in the Lord will renew their strength.
> They will soar on wings like eagles; they will run and not grow weary, they will walk and not be faint. *[Isaiah 40:31]*

It's a fact: Hope gives wings.

How does Dave's story help explain the way that hope in God gives strength and endurance even in tough times? What do I think of Dave's answer to the son's question? Would I have responded differently?

PRAYER

Lord, help me to see both the impermanence of my world and Your permanence. Help my hope increase as I think of my heavenly home.

Small Group Lesson 1

Hope Floats Your Boat

LEADER'S NOTE This study guide material is meant to be your servant, not your master. So please don't feel like you have to answer every question in each section before moving on; the point is to develop spiritually, not to check off every question as if this were a test. We recommend that group leaders review these questions before beginning in order to select those that you think will be most effective for your group. And if you want to try questions of your own, give them a whirl! We labeled some key questions with a **KEY** mark in each section. Just be sure to allow adequate time to pray and discuss the group assignment at the end of each meeting.

PARTICIPANT'S NOTE We encourage you to look over these questions before your group meets so that you'll be prepared for group discussion. You may even want to jot down some notes about how you might answer these questions. However, please do not feel limited to sharing only what you have written, and please do not feel disqualified to share if you have not written down responses!

CONNECT

1. **KEY** Go around the room and briefly introduce yourself to the other members of your group. How did you come to be a part of this group?

2. In this series we want to strengthen your sense of hope! Would you say that you tend to be hopeful or negative — are you a pessimist or an optimist? What would your friends say about you?

3. As we embark on this journey to experience biblical hope, how do you hope to change? In other words, what are your expectations of this Hope Experience?

As we affirm God's truth from the Bible, our thoughts change, leading to naturally transformed attitudes and positive actions. Often we try to start life change at the action level, but real change begins with knowing the Truth, and then the Truth will set you free!

This diagram represents the process of *spiritual transformation*. As we change our thinking, our attitudes are changed, and then our actions, and finally our whole selves, our lives, are made different... all because we have changed the way we think. This is what we hope to accomplish in this study!

4. At this point, allow anyone in the group to share anything that particularly challenged or encouraged them in last weekend's message or the daily Hope devotional readings. We'll begin each week's small group study with a chance to share reactions to that week's sermon and devotional readings.

WATCH THE VIDEO

✹ Available at www.HopeExperience.com or on DVD

We are in desperate need of hope!

- 23 million Americans suffer from anxiety disorders.
- 62 percent of evangelical Christians say they are worried about the future.

Biblical hope is the firm assurance that the problems of yesterday, today, and tomorrow will all work together in God's plan. It is a conviction that the best is yet to come. It is trust in the promises of God.

Some Promises of God

"For I know the plans I have for you," declares the Lord, "plans to prosper you and not to harm you, plans to give you hope and a future." *[Jeremiah 29:11]*

And we know that in all things God works for the good of those who love him, who have been called according to his purpose. *[Romans 8:28]*

...we will all be changed— in a flash, in the twinkling of an eye, at the last trumpet. For the trumpet will sound, the dead will be raised imperishable, and we will be changed. *[1 Corinthians 15:51b–52]*

Hope changes the way I see potential outcomes.

A person can endure anything so long as he has hope, for then he is walking not to the night but to the dawn. *William Barclay*

Hope changes the way I view life!

Hope changes the way I view suffering

I consider that our present sufferings are not worth comparing with the glory that will be revealed in us... For in this hope we were saved. But hope that is seen is no hope at all. Who hopes for what he already has? *[Romans 8:18,24]*

Hope changes the way I view death

Brothers, we do not want you to be ignorant about those who fall asleep, or to grieve like the rest of men, who have no hope. We believe that Jesus died and rose again and so we believe that God will bring with Jesus those who have fallen asleep in him. *[1 Thessalonians 4:13–14]*

WEEK

1

SMALL GROUP

✹ Hope changes the way I view myself

I pray that your hearts will be flooded with light so that you can understand the confident hope he has given to those he called — his holy people who are his rich and glorious inheritance! *[Ephesians 1:18 NLT]*

✹ Hope changes the way I view my future

"For I know the plans I have for you," declares the Lord, "plans to prosper you and not to harm you, plans to give you hope and a future." *[Jeremiah 29:11]*

✹ Hope changes the way I view God

Find rest, O my soul, in God alone; my hope comes from him. He alone is my rock and my salvation; he is my fortress, I will not be shaken. My salvation and my honor depend on God; he is my mighty rock, my refuge. Trust in him at all times, O people; pour out your hearts to him, for God is our refuge. *[Psalm 62:5–8]*

✹ Hope changes how I share my faith

But in your hearts set apart Christ as Lord. Always be prepared to give an answer to everyone who asks you to give the reason for the hope that you have. But do this with gentleness and respect, keeping a clear conscience, so that those who speak maliciously against your good behavior in Christ may be ashamed of their slander. *[1 Peter 3:15–16]*

✹ Hope changes what I live for

Command those who are rich in this present world not to be arrogant nor to put their hope in wealth, which is so uncertain, but to put their hope in God, who richly provides us with everything for our enjoyment. *[1 Timothy 6:17]*

ENGAGE

WEEK 1 SMALL GROUP

1. **KEY** Which do you identify with more, and why?

   - ❑ The sunken cement ship
   - ❑ A floating cement ship
   - ❑ A sailboat zipping along the waves
   - ❑ A becalmed sailboat sitting in a windless sea
   - ❑ The Titanic
   - ❑ The Love Boat
   - ❑ A tug boat
   - ❑ Other: ______________________________

2. Why do you suppose many Christians seem to have a weak hope — they can be negative and anxious — when the Bible says hope is to be one of the main characteristics of a Christian?

   - ❑ They read or watch too much negative news
   - ❑ They are exposed to too much negative media (music, movies, books, etc.)
   - ❑ They are unfamiliar with the biblical promises that inspire hope
   - ❑ They are undisciplined in their thought life, and allow despairing thoughts to take over
   - ❑ They may be predisposed to depression through no fault of their own
   - ❑ They have gone through so many negative experiences that they are in despair
   - ❑ They do not have positive Christian friendships that infuse them with hope
   - ❑ They are not aware that Christians are to be hope-filled people
   - ❑ They think it's more cool to be cynical than hopeful
   - ❑ Other: ______________________________

3. Which of the statements above applies to your own life?

WEEK

1

SMALL GROUP

4. How susceptible are you to negative influences from the media or from friends?

   ❏ **Very**: If I read a paranoid thriller, for example, it keeps me up with worries.

   ❏ **Somewhat**: I have to turn off the news after a while because it starts to depress me.

   ❏ **Not at all**: I seem to be able to absorb the most disturbing content without it affecting me… yet!

5. How does this susceptibility affect your hope level?

6. What does this suggest to you about steps you might need to take to increase your hope level?

7. Take a few minutes to chart your **hope level** on a graph. From childhood to today, chart your life's high and low Hope points.

8. After you are done with your chart, take some time to go around your group and explain your graph. If your group is larger than about eight people, break into smaller groups of three or four. What key incidents in your life took hope from you? What incidents made you more hopeful?

9. **KEY** In this seven-week study, we'll look at four areas that determine your hope level:

    - What is my view of God?
    - What is my view of myself?
    - What are my expectations of the future?
    - What is the outcome of suffering?

    In which one of these areas do you think you need to grow the most right now?

10. **KEY** Read the verses under **"Some Promises of God"** on page 11 out loud in your group. Which of these promises is particularly helpful for you, at this point in your life?

11. How do you think these promises, sincerely believed, would make a difference in someone's hope level?

12. How would you say biblical hope differs from the way the world uses the term "hope"?

APPLY

1. KEY Now think about a current situation you are facing. In what area of your life would you like to have more hope? Be as specific as you can, as long as you feel comfortable sharing.

   I would like to have more hope...

   - ❑ About my children
   - ❑ About my marriage
   - ❑ About getting married
   - ❑ About my future
   - ❑ About my relationship with ______________________
   - ❑ About ever changing myself
   - ❑ About my children's future
   - ❑ About my country's future
   - ❑ About the world's future
   - ❑ About my financial situation
   - ❑ About my work situation
   - ❑ About my relationship with God
   - ❑ Just generally about life; I tend to be negative and pessimistic
   - ❑ Other: ______________________________

2. How would real biblical hope impact your hope level in those areas of life you checked above?

3. René said, "We all live in a culture that is bombarding us with invitations to put our hope in exactly the wrong stuff; in our skills, in our deodorant, in our cars, jobs, looks, material possessions, wealth. But that is all temporary. It will all let you down." How do you see this to be true in the world around you?

4. How are you tempted to misplace your hope?

5. If you allowed that temptation to take hold, how would that negatively impact your perspective and how you live?

6. **KEY** What step will you take this week to allow hope to transform how you live?

   - ❑ Read the daily devotions
   - ❑ Memorize the verse of the week
   - ❑ Stay in touch with my small group members
   - ❑ Bring all my anxieties to God in prayer each morning and evening
   - ❑ Other practical ideas:

7. **KEY** Commit as a group that for the next 50 days you will allow God's words of hope to change your thinking by concentrating on them daily, and being faithful to attend small group and church together as much as possible.

8. One of the best ways to build a sense of hope in others is to tell them you are praying for them. Share your prayer requests with your small group.

9. **KEY** Specifically, ask for prayer that your sense of hope would grow in a particular part of your life. How would you finish this prayer?

   "Lord, may my sense of hope grow in this area of my life: __________
   ____"

   Share this with your group.

✹ For the future:

Throughout this study, record your group's prayer requests on page 109 of this book. Pray for one another throughout the week!

Close by having one group member pray that in the weeks to come God will bring new hope to every member of your group, and that the members of your group will be a part of making that happen.

WEEK

1

SMALL GROUP

BEFORE YOU LEAVE

KEY Take a few minutes to talk about where and when you will meet next week, and who will be in charge of any meals or snacks.

KEY Collect phone numbers and email addresses from your group members. The small group roster on page 108 is a good place to keep this information. Just pass the books around and have each member fill in their contact info.

Select one volunteer from your group to be the Email Coordinator… he or she can help forward prayer requests around the group, and send out reminders each week about the next meeting.

WEEK 2

THE FOUNDATION OF HOPE: MY VIEW OF GOD

May your unfailing love rest upon us, O Lord, even as we put our hope in you. *[Psalm 33:22]*

DAY

8

SUNDAY

by René Schlaepfer

My View of God

> MAY YOUR UNFAILING LOVE REST UPON US, O LORD, EVEN AS WE PUT OUR HOPE IN YOU. *[Psalm 33:22]*

One of my favorite places in the world is the British Museum in London. There you'll find the Rosetta Stone, the ancient Gates of Nineveh, Cleopatra's jewelry... and something that looks like a classic old pirate's map.

It's an ancient mariner's chart, drawn in 1525, outlining the east coast of North America. At that time most of the continent was unexplored — so the cartographer made some intriguing notes on areas of the map that were unknown: He wrote, in florid script, sayings like: "Here be giants!" "Here be fiery scorpions!" and "Here be dragons!"

Eventually the map came into the possession of Sir John Franklin, a British explorer from the late 1700s. He scratched out each of those fearful statements, and in their place wrote these words: "Here is God."

That says it all. What lies in store for you along the "unexplored coastlines" of your life — and your death? Well, for you, that's all unexplored country, and so it's tempting to be afraid. Maybe you even stay awake at night imagining the worst about your future ("Here be dragons!").

But you can scratch out the fears and write, "Here is God!" Here is the God of the Bible — the God identified as:

> The Provider *[Genesis 22:13–14]*
> The Mighty One *[Psalm 91:1]*
> The Ever-Present One *[Ezekiel 48:35]*
> My Shepherd *[Psalm 23:1]*
> The One Who Sees *[Genesis 16:13]*
> My Deliverer *[Romans 11:26]*
> My Rock *[Psalm 18]*

Now, if you're unsure about God's character, you'll be just as uneasy about Him as you are about the unknown future. But the more you know what the Bible teaches about God, the more confident you'll be as you think, "Here is God!" That's why this week we focus on the question, "Who is God?" As a hope exercise, read the descriptions in the list above every day this week, and each day add another biblical description of God to the list.

If I mapped out my worries about the future, where would I write something like, "Here be dragons"? Do I generally feel confident or uneasy as I think about my future? How does my view of God impact this?

PRAYER

Lord, help me to trust in You as my Rock even when I am unsure about what my future holds!

Hope in Who?

DAY
9
MONDAY
by Laurie Schlaepfer

✹ *Read Psalm 146:5*

The most quoted campaign slogan in the 2008 presidential election was *Got Hope?* It seemed to capture a longing many people of every political party had that year: An upwelling of desire, of *hope*, that we might find a human leader to solve all our nations' woes. Pundits on both sides talked about a messianic fervor. Even Barack Obama joked, "Contrary to the rumors you have heard, I was not born in a manger."

Of course this isn't a new phenomenon. Since the dawn of humanity, people have looked with hope to charismatic, visionary, or powerful men — kings, princes, generals, revolutionaries, rabbis, popes, pastors, governors, presidents, or mutual fund managers! Sometimes human leaders do great things to benefit the people they govern, but just as often they deeply disappoint. Regardless, it's foolish to place the full weight of our *Hope* (with a capital "H") on a human leader.

How have I placed too much hope in a mere human: a politician, a pastor, a teacher, a girlfriend or boyfriend, even the ideal of a husband or wife?

As C.S. Lewis writes:

> Never, never pin your whole faith [or hope] on any human being; not if he is the best and wisest in the whole world. There are lots of nice things you can do with sand; but do not try building a house on it.

PRAYER

Lord, help me redirect my Hope away from people and toward You!

Psalm 146 reminds us that even powerful people are ultimately powerless. They certainly can't save me, because they are powerless to save themselves from the destiny of all mankind — the grave. As the prophet Isaiah concurs:

> [God] brings princes to naught and reduces the rulers of this world to nothing. No sooner are they planted, no sooner are they sown, no sooner do they take root in the ground, than he blows on them and they wither, and a whirlwind sweeps them away like chaff. *[Isaiah 40:23–24]*

Only the Immortal One can ultimately save me. He is the Maker of the heavens and the earth, the One who sustains the universe and all life, the Faithful One. He *actually* has the power to right all wrongs, solve all problems, and make all things new. And He has *already* conquered the grave. Compared to the Lord, the most powerful "prince" looks like a little child playing dress up!

DAY

10

TUESDAY

by Jim Josselyn

Hope Not in Hercules

A HORSE IS A VAIN HOPE FOR DELIVERANCE;
DESPITE ALL ITS GREAT STRENGTH IT CANNOT SAVE.
BUT THE EYES OF THE LORD ARE ON THOSE WHO FEAR HIM,
ON THOSE WHOSE HOPE IS IN HIS UNFAILING LOVE...
[Psalm 33:17–18]

Read Psalm 33:16–21

Growing up in Santa Cruz, I attended a high school where I loved playing football. It was my passion and the one sport I seemed to excel in. Unfortunately, our high school was never known as a football powerhouse. It always seemed our rivals had more talent and bigger players. That is, until the year we received a transfer student from Southern Cal. His name was Joe, but we called him *Hercules*.

Joe was huge! He was a cross between Big Foot and Mr. T.

Joe was strong! He could bench press 350 pounds.

How could we lose with Joe on our side? We all imagined ourselves lofting high the state football championship trophy. Then reality set in as we entered the summer practice schedule. You see, although Joe was strong, he was also directionally challenged. He couldn't remember which way to run and collided with our quarterback a number of times. Our dreams for the season were dashed! We all realized we'd placed our hope in the wrong person.

How about you? Have you ever placed your hope in the wrong person or thing? It's an easy mistake to make. It's so common for me to shift the attention of my hope from the source of real hope (God), to my physical resources. Like so many, I was caught up in worry during the 2008 stock market crash. I started to play the worst case game in my head, the one that goes like this: "What would I do if: I lost my job, my house, or my health insurance?" I started dwelling on these scenarios and hope drained out of me. Then I remembered how the Apostle Paul begins most of his letters in the New Testament with the greeting: "Grace and peace to you from God our Father and the Lord Jesus Christ." When Paul wrote these letters, the church had plenty of things to worry about, plenty of things to rob them of their hope and joy. But in the midst of the turmoil they focused on the Lord. Today's verses remind us to look beyond our outward resources and look to God, to place our hope in Him and his strength.

Who — or what — has been my "Hercules"? What steps will I take today to strengthen my hope in Christ?

PRAYER

Dear Lord, I want to hope in You. Please remind me through the day to turn to You first.

Two Things That Bring Hope!

DAY

11

WEDNESDAY

by Mark Hillenga

FIND REST, O MY SOUL, IN GOD ALONE, MY HOPE COMES FROM HIM... *[Psalm 62:5]*

✸ *Read Psalm 62:1–12*

Katuk waited for the gigantic 100' wall of water to reach his small fishing boat just off the coast of northern Sumatra. Taking a deep breath, he dove in the water as the wave swept overhead. As he swam toward the surface with all his strength, he could feel the current hurling him towards shore. Finally reaching the surface, Katuk grabbed a palm tree branch as the water slowed and then began its retreat back towards the shoreline, bringing with it tons of swirling debris. As he surveyed the scene 80 feet below his perch in the palm tree, Katuk could see the ravaged coastline 1.5 miles away as the second wave began to come on shore.

Nine months later, Katuk and I stood looking at the Indonesian coast which was still stripped clear from the beach to the mountains by the 2004 tsunami. I asked him how he was coping with the loss of his wife and son to the tsunami. "God must have willed it. I must accept it," he said blankly.

I saw my friend's grief, and asked myself, "When does hope and trust in the sovereignty and power of God turn into mere resignation and despair?" It seemed to me that he had faith in a god of power, but that faith still led him to a hopelessness that tormented his very soul.

I really thought about this a lot, and was led to the conclusion that for my friend, "God" was really another word for "Fate." What's the difference between that and the God of the Bible?

In Psalm 62, verses 11 and 12 point out a very important truth: *"One thing God has spoken, two things have I heard: that you, O God, are strong,* AND *that you, O Lord, are loving."* **God is strong and God is loving.** Knowing only a God of strength can lead to the kind of hopelessness I saw in Katuk's eyes. God's strength coupled with His amazing love for us is what really leads to a hope that brings soul-rest. He is not just an impersonal force, unmoved by my tears and frustrations. You might say our world today is ravaged by a sin tsunami. God promises to care for us now, and one day to remake the world so there are no more tears. This is Christian hope.

Is there an area of hopelessness in your life right now? Rest in God alone, in the light of His power AND His love for you!

How could trust in God's sovereignty turn into a cold fatalism? How does Jesus show me not just God's power, but also His love?

PRAYER

Thank You, God, that You are powerful and loving.

DAY

12

THURSDAY

by René Schlaepfer

Hope in God, Not in Myths

> We have put our hope in the living God, who is the Savior of all men, and especially of those who believe.
> *[1 Timothy 4:10b]*

Read 1 Timothy 4:7–10

Is *hope* just another word for *gullibility*?

In today's passage, Paul emphatically says, "No." He tells us to have "nothing to do" with myths and tall tales. Apparently Christians were already turning to false sources of hope in the early church. Historians tell us about first-century Christian sects that taught of "mysteries" initiates could use to prophesy the future and control the spirits.

Why do "myths" have such novelty and appeal for so many? Am I placing my hope in a fad, myth, or novel teaching, or solely in God and His Word?

PRAYER

Lord, help me see if I am placing my hope on a passing fad or even a myth. Let me set my hope fully on You.

It happens to this day; in the name of faith, snake oil is still peddled. From the excesses of the prosperity movement ("Just believe in faith, and that new Mercedes is yours!") to new revelations about the end times ("Jesus is coming back in 2012!") to odd personal prophecies ("God has a word for you: Plastics.") to strange new diets ("Eat the raw Bible whole grain Garden of Eden program") to rituals and trinkets ("Use this prayer cloth and whatever you ask will come true!"), many of these teachings are not found in Scripture yet promise guaranteed results. Paul had a word for them: *Myths.*

Last year a friend of mine asked if I'd heard about the California hitchhiker who told some people just the previous week that Jesus was coming soon, and then vanished! I said, yes, I had heard about it. Thirty years ago. Our faith has no place for such urban legends.

It's sad that many Christians set all caution aside and believe everything they hear, especially if it comes from a teacher who has a magnetic personality or well-known ministry. They are destined for dashed hopes. Instead, train yourself to be disciplined in your beliefs. Set your hope fully on the living God, as revealed in the Bible.

The fads and trinkets of "voodoo Christianity" will come and go, but a simple hope in the One True God will endure. How do I tell the difference? I need to soak myself in Scripture, just as we're doing in this study!

Hope in the Source, Not the Resource

DAY
13
FRIDAY
by René Schlaepfer

Do any of the worthless idols of the nations bring rain? Do the skies themselves send down showers? No, it is you, O Lord our God. Therefore our hope is in you, for you are the one who does all this. *[Jeremiah 14:22]*

As a child, Bill Wilson experienced the hopelessness of abandonment. "One day, as I walked down a street with my mother, we stopped to sit for a while," he says. "She told me to sit there and wait for her to return." Bill waited for 3 days. She never came back. A Christian man who saw Bill sitting there stopped to help him... and changed Bill's life with a message of hope.

Out of his own experience with hopelessness, Bill developed a heart of compassion for at-risk children. In 1980 he founded a church in one of Brooklyn's roughest neighborhoods, known for its gangs, crime, drugs, and poverty.

Over the years, Pastor Bill has been beaten, stabbed and shot. Donations have at times dried up because of the seeming hopelessness of the mission. But his perseverance paid off: Crime levels have dropped, 22,000 children now experience the ministry of the church, and his influence on the neighborhood has been featured on programs like *Nightline*.

But how did he endure through the tough times? As he puts it, **"You have to hope in the source, not the resource."**

You have resources for accomplishing your God-given mission. Yet your resources can — and do — let you down at times. Christ-followers often make the subtle shift from really trusting in God to trusting in other Christians, trusting in their church, trusting in their knowledge, trusting in their own strength. Then when those things disappoint, they wrongly believe God let them down.

If you put your hope in the *resource*, you will inevitably be disappointed. But the *source*, God Himself, will never disappoint.

In what way am I struggling with hoping in my resources? How can I shift my focus to the Source: God?

PRAYER

Lord, free me from hoping in my resources. Thank You for being the True Source of all my hope!

DAY

14

SATURDAY

by Valerie Webb

Hope in What's Certain

COMMAND THOSE WHO ARE RICH IN THIS PRESENT WORLD NOT TO BE ARROGANT NOR TO PUT THEIR HOPE IN WEALTH, WHICH IS SO UNCERTAIN, BUT TO PUT THEIR HOPE IN GOD, WHO RICHLY PROVIDES US WITH EVERYTHING FOR OUR ENJOYMENT. *[1 Timothy 6:17]*

Read 1 Timothy 6:6–10 & 6:17–19

At first, you may wonder what these verses have to do with hope. Well, in some way, we all struggle with placing our hope in something other than God. When we place our hope in money we think it will get us out of trouble, will solve our problems, will help our relationships... but Paul says that is a trap.

In what ways do I struggle with placing my hope in money? How would that struggle change if I put my hope in God?

He should know: From what we know of Paul's background, it is reasonable to expect that he knew something of wealth. He was a Roman citizen, educated by a famous scholar, comfortable among merchants and politicians. We also know from scripture that Paul knew what it was to possess nothing. He went through times of absolute poverty.

PRAYER

Lord, thank You for all You've richly provided for me. I acknowledge that it is a blessing from You.

Focus on verse 17 for a moment. Paul says, *"To command those who are rich in this present world..."* Believe it or not, you and I are rich. You may not feel rich, but all you have to do is read the paper or watch the news to find out that there is a level of poverty in the world that we do not experience here in the States. So this verse is for each one of us.

Paul goes on to tell us not be arrogant (a side effect of thinking we *deserve* the blessing of money or we *earned* this money) and, *"...not to put their hope in wealth which is so uncertain..."* Well, the last year has been a huge lesson in the truth of that. Money comes and money goes, and lately it just goes!

Paul says instead to *"...put their hope in God, who richly provides us with everything for our enjoyment."* I love this! Paul doesn't just tell us to trust God; he reminds us that we are putting our hope in a *good* God, a God *"who richly provides"* for each of us and wants us to enjoy what He has provided. This is easy to read, but hard to do. We are all wrapped up in money in some way. How refreshing to release our grip on money and hope in God, watching Him provide for each need.

Small Group Lesson 2

WEEK
2
SMALL GROUP

The Foundation of Hope: My View of God

LEADER'S NOTE Please review these questions before beginning in order to select those that will be most meaningful and effective for your group. Do not feel obligated to answer them all. But please try to discuss at least one from each section, especially the **KEY** questions, allowing adequate time for prayer and to discuss the group assignment.

CONNECT

1. **KEY** What caught your attention, challenged or encouraged you in the weekend message or the devotionals?

2. Talk about a time when you had a wrong first impression of someone. What caused your impression to change?

3. If you asked people on the street to describe their image of God, what kind of answers would you get?

4. **KEY** Before you watch the video, turn in your Bibles to Psalm 103 and prepare to follow along.

WATCH THE VIDEO

We could take eternity to describe God's attributes, but today let's discuss ten aspects of God's personality that many people have difficulty believing.

The personality of God

Look at Psalm 103:2–14.

What can I learn about God just from this one passage?

1. God is ______________________________ with me

2. God is ______________________________ to me

WEEK

2

SMALL GROUP

3. God is ______________________________ to me

4. God is ______________________________ to me

5. God is ______________________________ to me

> The Lord your God is with you,
> He is mighty to save.
> He will take great delight in you,
> He will quiet you with his love,
> He will rejoice over you with singing. *[Zephaniah 3:17]*

What can I learn about God just from this passage?

6. God is ______________________________ me

7. God ______________________________ in me

8. God ______________________________ me

9. God ______________________________ over me

10. God ______________________________ about me

ENGAGE

1. Where do you think most people in our culture get their ideas about God?

- ❏ Greek and Roman mythology
- ❏ The Bible
- ❏ Movies
- ❏ Church
- ❏ Friends
- ❏ Imagination
- ❏ Childhood songs and stories
- ❏ Star Wars, Star Trek, and The Matrix!
- ❏ Other: ______________________________

2. **KEY** What image of God did you develop growing up? Where do you think it came from?

3. **KEY** Review the list of 10 aspects of God's personality from the video. Which are the easiest for you to believe, and which are the hardest?

4. Share a part of Psalm 103 that particularly hits home for you.

GROUP EXERCISE

1. **KEY** Read the following truths about God out loud, going around the room as each person reads one statement.

Some Biblical Truths About God

- God is patient with me and available to me. *[2 Peter 3:9]*
- God is kind and gracious and sympathizes with my weakness. He chooses to bring help to me. *[Psalm 103:8–12]*
- God loves me not because I have done anything to earn His love, but simply because He is gracious and forgiving. Even my faith in Christ is a gift from Him. *[Ephesians 2:8–9]*
- God forgives me for my sins and failures and does not hold them against me. When I have done wrong I can come to Him in openness and honesty knowing He has chosen to forgive me. *[1 John 1:9]*
- God accepts me regardless of my performance. He understands my weaknesses. *[Psalm 103:13,14]*
- God will work all things out for my good. I can trust Him. *[Romans 8:28]*
- God values me as His child. He is constantly affirming me and building me up. I have value because He created me and I am in Christ. *[John 1:12, 1 John 3:1–3]*
- God is reliable and is with me always, giving me fresh forgiveness every day. He will stick by me and support me *[Lamentations 3:22–23]*
- God is just, holy, and fair. He will treat me fairly and when He disciplines me, it will be done in love and for my own good. *[Hebrews 12:5–8]*

Adapted from Bill and Kristi Gaultiere's book, "Mistaken Identity'

WEEK
2
SMALL GROUP

2. **KEY** How did it make you feel to read these statements out loud?

3. How do you think a person's hope level changes if they believe these truths at their core level?

4. **KEY** In what way do you think your view of God tends to get distorted? In what way do you think it might be distorted now?

5. Take time now to complete this exercise individually. Don't answer the way you feel you *should*; be authentic. Don't answer from a *theological* perspective; this is about how you actually *feel*...

To what degree do I feel that God is like this toward me?					
	Never	Rarely	Sometimes	Often	Always
Gentle					
Harsh					
Loving					
Aloof					
Sympathetic					
Unconcerned					
Close					
Distant					
Kind					
Angry					
Supportive					
Demanding					
Gracious					
Provider					
Ignores me					
Rejoicing over me					
Consistent					
Unpredictable					
Just					
Unfair					
Chart adapted from Norman Wright's *Tomorrow Can Be Different*					

6. Share your answers to the following questions about the chart with your group:

   - Which words do I feel God is "often" or "always" like?
   - Which words do I feel God is "hardly ever" or "never" like?
   - What insights does this exercise reveal about my current image of God?

APPLY

Every day we face situations or forks in the road that demand us to make decisions influenced by what we believe about God. A biblically accurate view of God is an important part of having a life filled with hope.

1. **KEY** Share with your group a situation in your life that would be helped if you believed these truths about God, instead of your old distorted images of God.

2. How might your life would be different a year from now if you decided to believe these truths about God?

3. **KEY** What step will you take this week to help ensure that those 10 truths about God transform how you live? You can select more than one, or jot down your own idea:

   - ❏ Reread this section of the study guide each day this week
   - ❏ Memorize the list on page 29 and remind myself of it throughout each day
   - ❏ Look up the verses next to the statements and read at least one a day
   - ❏ Make a pact with a friend to call or email (or text!) each other with one of these truths as reminders each day this week
   - ❏ Pray through the lists of truths about God each day as a prayer of thanksgiving to God
   - ❏ Other: ______________________________

4. How can we as a group help you this week?

WEEK 2 SMALL GROUP

ACTION

Make plans to write group encouragement notes at the end of the next two week's meetings. Think of people who probably don't get enough encouragement:

- ❏ Politicians
- ❏ Public safety workers (policeman, fireman, teachers)
- ❏ Church staff or volunteers
- ❏ Teachers
- ❏ Shut-ins

Be thinking of who you'll write cards for; you can finalize your decision next week. Decide now who will purchase or create the cards and bring them to the group, how the group will pay for the cards, etc.

GROUP PRAYER

KEY One of the best ways to build a sense of hope in others is to tell them you are praying for them. Share your prayer requests with your small group and then take time to pray together.

Record your prayer requests on page 109 of this book. Pray for one another throughout the week!

Close by having one group member pray that we would base our lives on a biblical image of God and live free from any old distortions.

BEFORE YOU LEAVE

Take a few minutes to talk about where and when you will meet next week, and who will be in charge of any meals or snacks.

WEEK 3

THE MOST COMMON THIEF OF HOPE

I pray also that the eyes of your heart may be enlightened in order that you may know the hope to which he has called you, the riches of his glorious inheritance in the saints, and his incomparably great power for us who believe... *[Ephesians 1:18–19a]*

DAY
15
SUNDAY
by René Schlaepfer

How Do I See Myself?

I PRAY ALSO THAT THE EYES OF YOUR HEART MAY BE ENLIGHTENED IN ORDER THAT YOU MAY KNOW THE *HOPE* TO WHICH HE HAS CALLED YOU, THE RICHES OF HIS GLORIOUS INHERITANCE IN THE SAINTS, AND HIS INCOMPARABLY GREAT POWER FOR US WHO BELIEVE. *[Ephesians 1:18–19a]*

A friend of mine got this card:

God created rivers,
God created lakes,
God created you, Bob,
Everyone makes mistakes.

It's funny, but the truth is, many of us feel like that! In fact, right now you might feel like a mistake, a loser, someone with no future hope. As Larry Crabb says, "Those who have never struggled with self-hatred cannot know how crippling a problem it can be — or how stubborn." Every minor flub or major mistake reinforces my belief: "I am bad."

Do I feel uncomfortable affirming something the Bible says is true of me? Why?

But don't let defeat define you. Let God's love define you.

In today's verses from Ephesians chapter 1, Paul prays that "the eyes of your heart" may see the hope to which God has called you. Part of that is understanding your identity in Christ. Throughout this chapter and the next, Paul outlines the things that are true about followers of Jesus:

I am blessed *[Ephesians 1:3]*
I am chosen *[1:4]*
I am holy and blameless in His sight *[1:4]*
I am adopted into His family *[1:5]*
I am forgiven and redeemed *[1:7]*
I am empowered *[1:19]*
I am destined for a great inheritance *[1:11–14]*
I am a masterpiece designed for great deeds *[2:10]*

As an exercise, **read these truths out loud each day this week.** When the eyes of your heart see who you are in Christ and what you are promised in Him, your sense of anticipation — your future hope — will bloom! That's our emphasis this week!

You are not defined by your defeats. You are defined by what God says about you!

PRAYER

Lord, thank You for lavishing Your blessings on me and guaranteeing my inheritance.

Who Am I?

DAY
16
MONDAY
by René Schlaepfer

> BUT YOU ARE A CHOSEN PEOPLE, A ROYAL PRIESTHOOD, A HOLY NATION, A PEOPLE BELONGING TO GOD, THAT YOU MAY DECLARE THE PRAISES OF HIM WHO CALLED YOU OUT OF DARKNESS INTO HIS WONDERFUL LIGHT. *[1 Peter 2:9]*

Read 1 Peter 2:9–12

Dave Roever was in Vietnam when he was burned all over his body by a phosphor grenade. After he woke up in a hospital burn unit, David knew he looked grotesque. He felt he was worthless to anyone and without a future.

Dave wasn't alone in his room. There was another man who had also been badly burned. When this man's wife visited, she took off her wedding ring, put it on the nightstand, and said, "I'm so sorry, but there's no way I could live with you now. We are over." And she walked out the door. That soldier shook with tears for hours. Within two days, he died.

Three days later, Dave's wife arrived. After seeing what had happened with the other soldier, Dave had been dreading her visit. But his wife, a strong Christian with a great sense of humor, kissed him on the only place on his face that wasn't bandaged, and then said, "Frankly, Dave, in some ways, this is an improvement." Then she smiled and added, "Honey, I love you. I'll always love you. We are going to get you on your feet and out of here!" Within weeks Dave was healthy and out of the hospital. The difference between the two men? One word: *Hope*. Dave went on to speak all over the world, bringing to others the hope he found in Christ.

You may feel physically or spiritually ugly and worthless. You may have even had to endure rejection from loved ones. But in today's passage, God's Word says of all those who trust in Him: You are a chosen people. You are a royal priesthood. You are a holy nation. You are a people belonging to God. You have received mercy. You have a purpose: to declare the praises of Him who called you out of darkness into His wonderful light!

A woman emailed me: "I used to secretly refer to myself as 'the daughter of calamity.' With an abusive past and what looked like a short lifespan ahead, I thought of myself that way for years. Well, Jesus has been doing some extensive remodeling lately, and there is no place left in my soul for this kind of thinking. I am beginning to think there is a purpose for me. I need a new 'secret name' for myself." I emailed back: "How about we rechristen you 'Hope'?"

How closely aligned is my own self-image and self-talk with what the Bible says is true of me? How does this affect my sense of hope?

PRAYER

Lord, help me to see myself and my future the way You see me!

DAY

17

TUESDAY

by René Schlaepfer

A key component of my hope level is how I see myself. When I speak to myself, am I more like Nicky's psychologist ("I'll never change!"), or more like Pastor Wilkerson ("I can do all things in Christ!")?

PRAYER

Lord, thank You that there is hope for me as I put my trust in Christ!

Christ in Me, the Hope of Glory

> To them God has chosen to make known among the Gentiles the glorious riches of this mystery, which is Christ in you, the hope of glory. *[Colossians 1:27]*

Read Colossians 1:24–27

Nicky Cruz was the leader of the toughest gang in New York. He grew up hopeless and hate-filled after a childhood of abuse at the hands of both parents. "I wanted to do to others what my mother did to me," Nicky says. "I used to say I felt good when I hurt people."

But when he was alone, he didn't feel so good. "Privately, when I was alone, loneliness became like a monster that crawled inside my chest and ate me up. I was twisting and fighting; I felt so lost."

Only two people claimed to see into Nicky's heart. "A psychologist told me about five times. 'There's a dark side in your life that nobody can penetrate. Nicky, you are walking straight to jail, the electric chair, and hell. **There's no hope.**'"

A pastor named David Wilkerson saw the darkness in Nicky's heart, too. But he risked his life to tell Nicky **there was hope.** "He told me: 'God has the power to change your life.' I started cursing loud," says Nicky. "I spit in his face, and I hit him." Wilkerson answered, "You could cut me up into a thousand pieces. Every piece will still love you."

Nicky and his gang showed up at one of Wilkerson's services. One by one, they gave their lives to Christ. Finally, Nicky himself turned to Jesus, drawn by the hope of a changed life. That day a change did begin in Nicky; today this former gang member is himself a minister to the gangs of New York. **He knows best what they need most: Hope.**

Nothing in Nicky Cruz' background would have given anyone hope that he could change. As Paul says in today's Scripture, **his only hope was in Christ, "the hope of glory."** That means that, when I open my life to Christ, I begin to see his power at work inside me, changing me. Those changes give me hope that one day I will be changed completely, glorified and transformed into the image of Christ.

Hope After a Fall

DAY

18

WEDNESDAY

by René Schlaepfer

✺ *Read Lamentations 3:17–33*

The guilt you feel after a fall can be crippling. You tell yourself over and over: "I messed up. I abused people's trust. I am flushing my life away."

Silicon Valley entrepreneur Bill Dallas found that out when he was convicted of grand theft embezzlement. He shares his story in the book *Lessons from San Quentin*. He was a new Christian from a hard partying background when he was sent to the toughest prison in California. Emotionally shattered, he spent hours on the cell floor curled into a fetal position, weeping. The shame of his crime led him to complete and utter despair.

Hope came from an unlikely source: Members of the "Lifers' Club." These hardened criminals had come to grips with who they were and what they had done, and had found hope in a Christian faith based both on the reality of their helplessness and a daily dependence on the power of God. One of the lifers helped Bill get a job sweeping the prison TV studio. He now had a purpose that got him up every day. He started to explore his new faith. And he eventually turned around his entire world view. Today he helms a Christian satellite ministry and shares his story openly.

When you read Lamentations 3:17–33, what phrases do you identify with? How does this bring you hope?

Bill summarizes what he learned about recovering from a fall in these simple phrases: "Embrace your trials; choose sustaining faith in God; get a biblical self-image; get rid of self-absorption; persevere until you 'get it'; find freedom in God's forgiveness. **And cling to hope.**"

PRAYER

Lord, thank You for forgiving me and loving me even though I have fallen. Help me not to compound my sin with self-pity and hopelessness. Thank You for Your mercies which are new every morning!

Of course, those principles are from the Bible. In the book of Lamentations, Jeremiah also weeps over the horrible emotional and physical consequences of sin. Then he remembers:

> "Yet this I call to mind and *therefore I have hope*: Because of the Lord's great love we are not consumed, for his compassions never fail." *[Lamentations 3:21–22]*

No matter how far you've fallen, God's compassion never fails. In fact, the entire Bible is an example of how God uses flawed and fallen people for great things: From Moses to David to Thomas to Paul, the saints we meet are error-prone and sinful. In other words, they're human. And the Bible makes their humanness plain to show God's power and to give hope to a despairing world.

DAY
19
THURSDAY
by René Schlaepfer

When God Makes a Valley into a Door

There I will give her back her vineyards, and will make the Valley of Achor a door of hope. *[Hosea 2:15a]*

✽ *Read Hosea 2:15–23*

In Hosea 2:15 God says *"I will make the valley of Achor a door of hope."* The Hebrew word *achor* means "trouble." So in the original language, God is saying, "I will make the valley of *trouble* into a door of *hope*."

What's the story behind that verse? In the book of Hosea, God talks about the wayward nation of Israel in a love poem, using the metaphor of marriage. He portrays himself as a loving husband, and Israel as a promiscuous wife. At this point in history Israel was abandoning worship of God for the idols of Baal, a cult that included ritual prostitution and drunkenness. "She went after lovers, but me she forgot," God sadly sings. He asks the reader to imagine the emotions of such a husband — there is anger and a sense of betrayal, but there is also love, and a longing for the beautiful woman he knows is hidden beneath the debauchery. God says this is how He yearns to be reunited with Israel — and with anyone who has abandoned him for sin.

How have I seen a "valley of trouble" turn into a "door of hope"? How does "hitting bottom" open my ears to God's voice again?

God's plan: To lead Israel away from the lush lands around the Jordan river and into the desert, the valley of Achor. This happened historically when the nation was booted into the wilderness by invading armies. As a people, they hit bottom. But God says that there, in the "Valley of Trouble," He will once again court His bride. *"I will speak tenderly to her… and I WILL MAKE THE VALLEY OF TROUBLE A DOOR OF HOPE."*

PRAYER

God, thank You for Your love for me even though I have been unfaithful to You. Help me see the door of hope in my valley of trouble.

Don't miss it: God is saying *it's that very trouble itself* that He will use as a door of hope. How many times have you prayed for loved ones, that God would show them their need of Him? So God leads them toward the Valley of Trouble. And then you want to step in and keep them from the valley!

Or how many times have you wondered if your own tough times were a sign God no longer loved you? But in fact they're a gift of love from God. It's when we hit bottom that we hear God's voice more clearly.

So if you feel you're living in Achor, don't give up! Look around: In that dark valley, there is a portal through which you will see blue skies again. Listen to God today as He whispers tender words of love to you from that doorway and woos you back to Him.

Envy vs. Hope

DAY

20

FRIDAY

by Valerie Webb

> Do not let your heart envy sinners,
> but always be zealous for the fear of the Lord.
> There is surely a future hope for you,
> and your hope will not be cut off. *[Proverbs 23:17–18]*

Have you noticed that so often when the Bible talks about hope it is an antidote to a problem?

In this passage the contrast is between envy and hope. On first glance you may think, "I don't envy sinners!"

That's what I thought too!

So let's think about this. Honestly, there are times when I'm struggling with a habitual sin so intensely that I am envious of those who don't care what God thinks. I imagine, "It would be so much easier to just give up and wallow in my own choices and desires."

I'm so grateful that God knew we'd have these moments. And what does He offer us in exchange for envy and wallowing in our sin? Hope: "*A future hope that cannot be cut off.*"

What's great about this hope is that hope in God can outlast any envy, any struggle, any temptation. Not because of the power of *your* hope, but because of the certainty of the *object* of your hope: God.

So when you are tempted to envy, whether it is your perception of someone else's freedom, someone's position or someone else's life, refocus your emotions on your unchanging God and the future hope He has for you.

When has envy robbed me of hope? How does knowing I have a future hope that cannot be taken away encourage me today?

PRAYER

Lord, I confess to You that there are times I envy others in these ways (think about this and confess specifically to God). Help me replace that envy with a confident hope in Your power and Your Word.

ACTION

In preparation for next weekend's "Spread Hope" emphasis, think of a way you can be an agent of hope this weekend!

DAY

21

SATURDAY

by Kevin Deutsch

What was my hope level like before I understood Christ's salvation? What is it like now?

PRAYER

Lord, thank You for bridging the gap so that I don't have to be separated from You. I need the hope offered me in Christ. I put my life entirely in Your hands!

ACTION

In preparation for next weekend's "Spread Hope" emphasis, spend time today doing a "Hope Project" (see the suggestions on page 111).

Once without Hope

> Remember that at that time you were separate from Christ, excluded from citizenship in Israel and foreigners to the covenants of the promise, without hope and without God in the world. *[Ephesians 2:12]*

The harbor water that morning was thick and gray under an overcast sky. I was 13 years old and stood next to my brother at the back of the boat, surrounded by some family and some strangers, all gathered to scatter the ashes of my Dad.

We slowly motored out of the harbor into the drab day. "Look," my mother said, "one of those sea gulls is following us; maybe it's the spirit of your Dad." It was an absurd thought, but I nodded vaguely, having no other comforting thoughts.

A generic eulogy was offered, but my Dad was an agnostic — what could really be said? The boat moved forward; ashes were scattered. A man threw a bouquet of flowers attached to a Styrofoam ring out onto the water. As he cast it out to sea, the wind flipped it over and it landed — flower side down — in the water behind the boat. Now, looking more like a floating toilet seat than anything else, I couldn't help but look at my brother and smile.

That was my first smile in two weeks, and though I had a brief sense of relief, I felt a more permanent sense of dread; I would die one day, like my Dad. Perhaps I'd be an alcoholic like him, too. Even though it was punctuated by a handful of happy distractions here and there, my life was dominated by hopelessness, paralleled by my anger at a father who drank himself to death and a God who would let him.

But at the age of 25, something happened. A Christian friend lent me a novel, and nestled in the pages was a simple yet profound explanation of the Gospel: That I would remain hopeless forever if I continued rejecting God, and that God's love was so great that Jesus would willingly go to the cross to take the punishment reserved for me. I prayed for the first time in twelve years, asking God, "Is this true?" And at once I experienced the tremendous joy and relief I had always sought! Above it all, there came a wonderful sense of *hope* as I stepped into communion with God, my true Father, eternal and perfect. As the next verse in Ephesians describes it:

> But now in Christ Jesus you who once were far off have been brought near by the blood of Christ. *[Ephesians 2:13]*

Small Group Lesson 3

WEEK
3
SMALL GROUP

The Most Common Thief of Hope: How I See Myself

LEADER'S NOTE: Please review these questions before beginning in order to select those that will be most meaningful and effective for your group. Do not feel obligated to answer them all. But please try to discuss at least one from each section, especially the **KEY** questions, allowing adequate time for prayer and to discuss the group assignment.

CONNECT

1. **KEY** What caught your attention, challenged or encouraged you in the weekend message or the devotionals?

2. Whether we consciously do it or not, we all have an image we like to portray to people. For example, some want to be seen as a gentle helper, a strong and smart leader that has it all together, or a fun-loving, easy-going guy that is the life of the party. How do you want others to see you?

3. **KEY** Read Ephesians 1:3–23 and 2:1–10 out loud (you can assign sections, or just have one or two group members read).

WATCH THE VIDEO

1. ____

> PRAISE BE TO THE GOD AND FATHER OF OUR LORD JESUS CHRIST, WHO HAS *BLESSED* US IN THE HEAVENLY REALMS *WITH EVERY SPIRITUAL BLESSING* IN CHRIST. *[Ephesians 1:3]*

2. ____

> FOR *HE CHOSE US* IN HIM BEFORE THE CREATION OF THE WORLD... *[Ephesians 1:4a]*

3. ______________________________

...to be *holy and blameless in his sight.* *[Ephesians 1:4b]*

4. ______________________________

In love he predestined us to be *adopted as his sons* through Jesus Christ, in accordance with his pleasure and will. *[Ephesians 1:5]*

5. ______________________________

In him we have *redemption* through his blood, *the forgiveness of sins*, in accordance with the riches of God's grace... *[Ephesians 1:7]*

6. ______________________________

Having believed, you were marked in him with a seal, the promised Holy Spirit, who is a deposit guaranteeing our inheritance until the redemption of those who are God's possession — to the praise of his glory. *[Ephesians 1:13–14]*

7. ______________________________

For we are God's *workmanship...* *[Ephesians 2:10a]*

8. ______________________________

...created in Christ Jesus *to do good works*, which God *prepared in advance* for us to do. *[Ephesians 2:10b]*

ENGAGE

1. KEY In what way do you sometimes have a distorted, fun-house mirror view of yourself or your worth? In other words, what are some of the "old tapes" you play about yourself that contain negative self-evaluations?

   - ❏ I think I can never change
   - ❏ I think I am unblessed or unlucky
   - ❏ It's hard to believe people would like me
   - ❏ I feel like I will make a fool of myself
   - ❏ I wonder if anyone really loves me for who I am
   - ❏ I feel like a fake
   - ❏ I feel like God is just waiting to punish me
   - ❏ I think I am not as spiritual or good as others think I am
   - ❏ I think I'm stupid
   - ❏ I think I'm clumsy
   - ❏ Other: ____

2. How did you get this view of yourself?

3. What do you think hinders people from seeing themselves the way God sees them?

   - ❏ Culture
   - ❏ Family
   - ❏ Friends
   - ❏ Themselves (Self-pity, etc.)
   - ❏ Ignorance
   - ❏ Other: ____

4. What is hindering you from seeing yourself the way God sees you?

5. Do you believe God loves you completely, just the way you are? Why or why not? What difference do you think really seeing yourself the way God sees you will make in your life?

6. Turn to page 10 in your book. Review the diagram of spiritual transformation. Remember that what we believe is the foundation for our hope. For an infusion of biblical hope, we have to choose God's image of ourselves.

7. Look at the verses you read from Ephesians. Which of the truths about your identity in Christ listed there particularly excites or inspires you?

8. **KEY** Take a moment to look at this list of how God sees you and rate yourself from 1 to 10, 1 being lowest. Of course these are all "10" biblically, but what we're asking you to do is to rate how you respond when you hear these truths: How much do you really believe these things are true of you? Then share your numbers with the group.

    _____ I am blessed

    _____ I am chosen

    _____ I am, in God's sight, holy and blameless

    _____ I am a child of God

    _____ I am forgiven

    _____ I am secure

    _____ I am a masterpiece

    _____ I have a God-designed destiny

    These truths about you are all **solid**, they are **unchangeable**, they are **non-erodible**, they are permanent because they are **dependent on God's grace**, not your good works. These truths are not based on what people think of you — this is not talking yourself into something. This is based on what God says about you.

9. What happens when you build your hope on your good works and performance and not on God's grace?

10. What happens to your hope when you care about the opinion of others more than God's opinion?

APPLY

1. **KEY** Have a member of your group read this paragraph:

   > The most common thief of hope is how I see myself. Yet at times we all feel unblessed, not chosen, unholy, guilty, unforgiven, messed up and without destiny. The biblical truth is that, in fact, we **are** all guilty of sin, and none of us can **earn** the blessing of God's love. But that's not the end of the matter. We also are intensely loved by God. He chooses to bless us with His love, not because we have earned it, but by His grace. He chooses to see us as holy and blameless. He will transform us into Christ-likeness as we surrender to Him. He has a great destiny planned for us.

   What are some signs that even a small distortion of the truth is robbing my hope?

GROUP EXERCISE

1. **KEY** Take some time to consider this question: What is a current situation in your life that is made worse by a weak or distorted, non-biblical view of yourself? Here are some options to get you thinking:

   - ❏ I have been putting off a dream God placed on my heart
   - ❏ I have been yielding to peer pressure
   - ❏ I've been tempted to give up on the idea of ever changing myself
   - ❏ I've been tempted to give up on the idea of ever changing a certain relationship
   - ❏ I have been depressed about my future
   - ❏ I've been allowing fears to get the better of me
   - ❏ Other: ______________________________

2. How does a weak view of your identity make that situation seem more hopeless?

3. Now take some time to individually complete the following exercise. Then share your completed sentence with your group:

Infuse at least one of the truths about your identity in Christ into the situation you thought of on the previous page, and fill in the blanks:

"In this situation:

____

(name a specific situation or struggle in your life here)

...I will make the decision to act on the truth that I am/have:

____

(name a truth about your biblical identity that relates to the situation)

... and choosing to believe this truth will create hopeful attitudes and positive actions."

---

4. What step can you take this week to allow these truths about your identity in Christ to transform how you view and bless others?

GROUP ACTIVITY

1. **KEY** Today, as a group, write at least one encouragement card to someone in the community. Let that light shine! You'll do this next week too.

2. **KEY** Looking ahead: Choose a group "Spread Hope" community project to do before your next group meeting! Some possibilities:

- ❏ Do a community outreach project through church
- ❏ Clean up a beach or river
- ❏ Clean up a local park or school
- ❏ Volunteer at a food bank or soup kitchen
- ❏ Visit a local nursing home, or a person you know who is a shut-in
- ❏ Partner with a jail ministry to start a Hope Experience group there
- ❏ Assist in a local HIV/AIDS outreach

There are more ideas about ways you can spread hope on page 111.

✸ Organize your group:

Who will bring what materials to your project site?

When and where will your group meet?

PRAYER

In what ways do you need to trust God for how you see yourself? What is one way your group can be praying for you as you take this new step of obedience?

KEY Share your prayer requests with your small group and then take time to pray together.

Record your prayer requests on page 109 of this book. Pray for one another throughout the week!

BEFORE YOU LEAVE

Take a few minutes to talk about where and when you will meet next week, and who will be in charge of any meals or snacks.

WEEK 4

SPREAD HOPE!

But in your hearts set apart Christ as Lord. Always be prepared to give an answer to everyone who asks you to give the reason for the hope that you have. But do this with gentleness and respect, keeping a clear conscience, so that those who speak maliciously against your good behavior in Christ may be ashamed of their slander. *[1 Peter 3:15–16]*

DAY

22

SUNDAY

by René Schlaepfer

Spreading Hope

THERE IS SURELY A FUTURE HOPE FOR YOU, AND YOUR HOPE WILL NOT BE CUT OFF. *[Proverbs 23:18]*

Management guru Ken Blanchard once led a training session for retail workers where he talked about the power of encouraging words.

About a month later, his office got a call from a man named Johnny, who said, "I was at your seminar. I'm nineteen. I have Down Syndrome. I work as a bagger at a grocery store and I liked your talk, but didn't know what I could do. Well, I got an idea. Every day I come up with a statement that's encouraging. If I can't find one in a quote book I have, I make it up. I print it out on 300 slips of paper." Johnny said he signs them all, and the next day puts them into his customer's bags as he says, "Here is something special for you!"

After another month Blanchard's office got another call, this time from Johnny's store manager who reported, "Something amazing is happening. We always have lots of check stands open, but the line where Johnny's bagging often goes all the way back to the frozen food section. A customer told one of our supervisors, 'I used to only shop once a week. Now I shop almost every day, just to get Johnny's quote!'"

After yet another month, the manager called again and said, "This is changing the entire culture of our store: Like, when a flower was broken, we used to just throw it away. Now I watch as our clerks pin those flowers onto elderly women or little girls just to brighten their day. People are looking for ways they can be like Johnny and give people some encouragement!"

Johnny the grocery bagger is speaking words of hope that are changing his store's culture. If it can happen at a grocery store, it can happen in your family, at your workplace, in your church. Speak words of hope! Look for ways your deeds can spread hope, too!

Today's verse is a great example: A father tells a son troubled by evildoers, "There is surely a future hope for you...." Simple, encouraging words and deeds backed up by scriptural promises will *change lives!*

This week we'll emphasize *spreading hope*. Of this you can be certain: Every single person you see needs a dose of hope today!

How can I spread hope through my words and deeds in specific ways this week?

PRAYER

Lord, help me be a channel of Your hope to everyone around me today!

Agents of Hope

...CONTINUE IN YOUR FAITH, ESTABLISHED AND FIRM, NOT MOVED FROM THE HOPE HELD OUT IN THE GOSPEL. *[Colossians 1:23a]*

DAY

23

MONDAY

by René Schlaepfer

Read Colossians 1:15–23

It's always easy to find prophets of doom.

Toward the end of his life, novelist H. G. Wells grew hopeless about the fate of the human race. He thought we'd inevitably destroy ourselves, having only "one thousand years more" to survive.

Former Secretary of State Henry Kissinger was widely quoted for this tongue-in-cheek remark:

> "More than at any time in history, mankind faces a crossroads — one path leading to despair and utter hopelessness, the other leading to total destruction. Let us pray we have the wisdom to choose correctly."

In contrast, **Christians are to be agents of hope to the world**, *"overflowing with hope" [Romans 15:13]*, people *"called to hope" [Ephesians 1:18]*, always ready to give *"reasons for our hope" [1 Peter 3:15]*, staying *"anchored in hope" [Hebrews 6:19]* as we trust the *"God of hope" [Romans 15:13]*. **To a dreary, doubt-filled, despairing world, we're to be a breath of fresh, hopeful air!**

Too bad a lot of Christians I know are hope-busters who seem to rejoice in doomsday predictions. They sound a lot more like H.G. Wells than the Apostle Paul! It's as if they believe it's more spiritual to be pessimistic than optimistic. That happens when we ignore Paul's warning in today's verse to *"...continue in your faith, established and firm,* ***NOT MOVED FROM THE HOPE HELD OUT IN THE GOSPEL.***"

What is the gospel hope? **Reread Colossians 1:15–23** for a further description of the spiritual reality that we often miss: Jesus is in ultimate control of history.

Now this doesn't mean I'm never sad. Hope goes beyond mere emotion. Hope is the confidence-giving certainty that springs from believing the promises of God that, ultimately, **every single thing that happens to me today will be used for good**, and **every single wrong will one day be set right.**

How and why do Christians move away from the hope held out in the gospel, and fall into despair? How can I stay focused on hope, and help others to do the same?

PRAYER

Lord, in a world of pessimism, help me to be a breath of hope to those around me!

DAY

24

TUESDAY

by René Schlaepfer

Building Hope in Others with My Words

Read 2 Corinthians 5:16–21

James S. Hewett writes about his son, who was using one of those super-adhesive glues on a model airplane: "In less than three minutes, his right index finger was bonded to a wing of his DC-10. He tried to free it. He tugged it, pulled, waved it frantically, but he couldn't budge his finger free." Eventually they found a solvent that freed his finger, and all was well. Then Hewett writes: "Last night I remembered that incident when I met a new family in our neighborhood. The father introduced his children: 'This is Pete. He's the clumsy one of the lot. That's Kathy coming in with mud on her shoes. She's the sloppy one. And, as always, Mike is last. He'll be late for his own funeral, I promise you.'"

Hewett goes on to say, "That dad did a thorough job of gluing his children to their faults and mistakes. People do it to us all the time. They remind us of our failures, our errors, our sins, and they won't let us live them down. Like my son trying frantically to free his finger from the plane, there are people who try, sometimes desperately, to free themselves from their past. They'd love a chance to begin again. When we don't let people forget their past, we glue them to their mistakes and refuse to see them as more than something they have done. However, when we forgive, we gently pry the doer of the hurtful deed from the deed itself..."

Part of spreading hope to others is speaking encouraging words to them, words that build hope. This doesn't mean you have to deny their faults; it means you reveal the truth about who they are, and what their potential is, in God's eyes.

A few days ago, we saw, in Ephesians 1, how the Apostle Paul is doing just that for the Ephesians. We know from Revelation 2 that the Ephesian church was, at least eventually, task-oriented and loveless. Yet Paul does not label them; he does not say, "Dear Frozen Chosen." He speaks words of hope. In today's verse he does the same for the Corinthians, who were undisciplined and worldly: *"So from now on we regard no one from a worldly point of view... if anyone is in Christ, he is a new creation; the old has gone, the new has come!"*

Today look for chances to build hope, not despair, into others with your words!

What will I say to specific people in my life to build hope in them today?

PRAYER

Lord, thank You for the truths about me revealed in Your Word. Help me to follow Paul's example and gently encourage others, seeing them as new creations in Christ!

Share Reasons for Your Hope

by René Schlaepfer

ALWAYS BE PREPARED TO GIVE AN ANSWER TO EVERYONE WHO ASKS YOU TO GIVE THE REASON FOR THE HOPE THAT YOU HAVE. BUT DO THIS WITH GENTLENESS AND RESPECT, KEEPING A CLEAR CONSCIENCE, SO THAT THOSE WHO SPEAK MALICIOUSLY AGAINST YOUR GOOD BEHAVIOR IN CHRIST MAY BE ASHAMED OF THEIR SLANDER. *[1 Peter 3:15b–16]*

✺ *Read 1 Peter 3:13–17*

This is one of my favorite verses in the Bible: *"Always be prepared to give a reason for your hope..."*

I love doing mental exercises — how would I explain my hope in Christ to *that* person?

For example, when I read a blog by someone who is obviously intensely secular or even anti-Christian, or when I drive past the Wiccan bookstore downtown, or when I ride my bike past the bar further down the street, I ask myself: If this blogger, or Wiccan, or partyer asked me to give the reasons for my hope, what would I say? How would I phrase it **gently and respectfully**, as Peter says, in ways they might relate to?

I've imagined starting with my childhood: "Losing my dad as a little kid made me long for a father. I finally found what I was looking for when I understood God as my Heavenly Father." Or I imagine saying, "I was burned out by religion, until I saw it this way: You could spell religion 'D-O'. Do. Do things. But you spell faith in Christ as 'D-O-N-E'. He has done it; He has paid the price for my sins. That sets me free." These little mental exercises have often turned into actual conversations... perhaps because I've been working out in my head what I might say. Of course the conversations never go exactly as I pretended. They are always more interesting than in my imagination, and require a lot of listening and sensitivity on my part so I can try to understand how to be respectful and reasonable to that specific person.

So let's do what this verse tells us to do: Think of one person who is not a believer: a real person, like a friend or even a celebrity. Imagine he or she asks, "Why are you so hopeful?" In the interest of *"always being prepared,"* answer the questions at right **as briefly and memorably as you can.**

Why am I hopeful? What difference has trust in Jesus made in my life?

PRAYER

Lord, help me to enjoy the exercise of always being prepared to share my hope with gentleness and respect. Please give me the opportunity this week to share my hope!

DAY
26
THURSDAY
by René Schlaepfer

The Effect of Hope

EVERYONE WHO HAS THIS HOPE IN HIM PURIFIES HIMSELF, JUST AS HE IS PURE. *[1 John 3:3]*

Read 1 John 3:1–3

Parade magazine told the amazing story of self-made millionaire Eugene Lang, who had been asked to speak to a class of 59 sixth-graders in East Harlem, New York. What could he say to inspire these students? Statistically, most of them would drop out of school to sell drugs or join gangs. In fact, he wondered how he could get these children to even look at him.

Tossing his notes aside, he decided to speak from his heart. "Stay in school," he said, "and I'll pay the college tuition for every one of you!" At that instant, the lives of those kids changed. **For the first time they had hope.**

As one student said, **"I had something to look forward to, something waiting for me. It was a golden feeling."** Nearly 90 percent of that class went on to graduate from high school and enter college, far above the normal rate for their peers.

Did you know you have a similar promise? Reread 1 John 3:1–3, where the writer explains that God the Father lavishes his love on us, his children, with the promise of a great gift on our "graduation day": We will be like Him, without sin. Theologians call it our "glorification." Then he says, *"everyone who has this hope PURIFIES himself."*

What does he mean, hope "purifies" us? Very much like what that student meant when he spoke of the motivation he got from Mr. Land's offer. When you're promised a bright future, you're inspired to endure, to do well, to say "no" to the demons that tempt you, and "yes" to the opportunities before you!

You too can say, "I have something to look forward to, something waiting for me." And you can inspire others with this same promise! **Hope really is a golden feeling!**

How does the idea of heavenly resurrection and reward motivate me?

PRAYER

Lord, thank You so much for lavishing love on me as one of Your children! Thank You for the promise of heavenly transformation — may this hope purify me in a very practical way here on earth!

Hold on to Hope

by Dan Baker

Let us hold unswervingly to the hope we profess, for he who promised is faithful. *[Hebrews 10:23]*

✺ *Read Hebrews 10:19–25*

My father exhibited confident hope in the midst of suffering with a lung disease that eventually took his life. One of his favorite songs was *This Old House* by Tennessee Ernie Ford. Dad knew his body, or *"his house,"* was wearing out. But he had hope, not in the things of this earth, but in the faithful promises of God. That's why he loved the lyrics, *"Ain't gonna need this house no longer, I'm a-gettin' ready to meet the saints."*

And Dad held on to this hope right up to his very last day as he sang with his grandchildren yet another of his favorites, *"Soon and very soon we are going to see the King."*

In today's verses the author of the book of Hebrews gives us four strong encouragements for our lives. He says, *"Let us draw near," "Let us hold unswervingly," "Let us consider,"* and *"Let us not give up."*

1. *"Let us draw near... to God"* — We need to stay close to God. Spend time with Him everyday. He is our only reliable source of hope.
2. *"Let us hold unswervingly... to the hope"* — We can hold on to hope because God is completely trustworthy. He will fulfill His promises.
3. *"Let us consider... one another"* — We need to pass this hope on to others, with good deeds as well as words!
4. *"Let us not give up... meeting together"* — We need to spend time with each other regularly. We are much more likely to hold on to hope when we experience the encouragement and support of others who also trust in God.

"The day is approaching" when the temporal things of this world will pass away. That is why we must hold on to hope in our faithful God.

In what area of my life do I need to "hold on to hope" today?

PRAYER

Lord, help me be a strength to others who need hope today.

DAY

28

SATURDAY

by Kevin Deutsch

What distracts me from seeing God as a Father who loves me?

PRAYER

Lord, I put my hope in Your unfailing love for me!

My Hope Pleases God

THE LORD DELIGHTS IN THOSE WHO FEAR HIM,
WHO PUT THEIR HOPE IN HIS UNFAILING LOVE. *[Psalm 147:11]*

Read Psalm 147

If my kids were to write a job description for me, I believe that the first bullet-point would read, *"Dad will give me whatever I want, whenever I want!"* Of course if I actually did give them everything they wanted, whenever they wanted it, none of them would be alive.

As their father, I know what they really need. I don't let our youngest son toddle across the street to go the park. I don't let our 4-year-old daughter "do the cooking like Mama does" and grab the pot of boiling water off the stove. And our oldest son, who's in junior high — well, I believe that speaks for itself! If I allowed my children to do whatever they wanted, the results would be disastrous.

The real job description should read, *"Dad will take care of me whenever I need it, because he loves me."* I love being the go-to guy when things go wrong in their lives. When my child gets a scraped knee, it fills me with joy to console them, clean them up, and — like the psalmist writes — *"bind up their wounds."*

In the moments they really believe this to be true, and show it — those times they lean on me and hug me with total belief in my love for them — I am delighted. My heart sings for joy when they fall asleep secure in my arms or even simply look at me with relaxed trust.

I believe this blueprint of good fatherhood comes from our Father in Heaven: *"He delights in those who put their hope in His unfailing love."* When we crawl into his lap in complete hope and trust, He is blessed.

Just think: There is something you can do to bring delight to the God of the Universe! And as verse 10 implies, it's not a spectacular deed or showy accomplishment. It's simple hope in who He is and His unfailing love for you — that every moment of every day, God loves you more than you can even imagine! Bring delight to your Father today!

Small Group Lesson 4

WEEK
4
SMALL GROUP

Building Hope in Others

LEADER'S NOTE Please review these questions before beginning in order to select those that will be most meaningful and effective for your group. Do not feel obligated to answer them all. But please try and discuss at least one from each section especially the **KEY** questions. Make sure you allow adequate time for prayer and to discuss the next group assignment.

CONNECT

1. **KEY** What caught your attention, challenged or encouraged you in the weekend message or the devotionals?

2. **KEY** Share your experiences from your "Spread Hope" project if you did one this past week. What did you do? How was your own sense of hope impacted? Did you get any positive feedback?

3. In preparation for today's study on spreading hope, describe a time when you were particularly encouraged by someone in your life. It could be a teacher, a coach, a pastor, a friend. Briefly share the circumstances and how it made you feel.

WATCH THE VIDEO

Spreading Hope

The Greek word for *"one another"* is used more than 100 times in the New Testament! Some examples:

> Carry each other's burdens, and in this way you will fulfill the law of Christ. *[Galatians 6:2]*

> Therefore encourage one another and build each other up, just as in fact you are doing. *[1 Thessalonians 5:11]*

> Accept one another, then, just as Christ accepted you, in order to bring praise to God. *[Romans 15:7]*

> Be kind and compassionate to one another, forgiving each other, just as in Christ God forgave you. *[Ephesians 4:32]*

WEEK
4
SMALL GROUP

✸ How can I build hope in the lives of people around me?

1. Make ______________________________ my central hope each day

> …SET YOUR HOPE FULLY ON THE GRACE TO BE GIVEN YOU WHEN JESUS CHRIST IS REVEALED. *[1 Peter 1:13b]*

2. Let the Word of Christ ____________________________ in me richly

> LET THE WORD OF CHRIST DWELL IN YOU RICHLY AS YOU TEACH AND ADMONISH ONE ANOTHER WITH ALL WISDOM, AND AS YOU SING PSALMS, HYMNS AND SPIRITUAL SONGS WITH GRATITUDE IN YOUR HEARTS TO GOD. *[Colossians 3:16]*

3. Watch what I _____________________________________ to others

> DO NOT LET ANY UNWHOLESOME TALK COME OUT OF YOUR MOUTHS, BUT ONLY WHAT IS HELPFUL FOR BUILDING OTHERS UP ACCORDING TO THEIR NEEDS, THAT IT MAY BENEFIT THOSE WHO LISTEN. *[Ephesians 4:29]*

> THERE IS SURELY A FUTURE HOPE FOR YOU, AND YOUR HOPE WILL NOT BE CUT OFF. *[Proverbs 23:18]*

4. Creatively ____________________________ for ways to build hope

> WE WHO ARE STRONG OUGHT TO BEAR WITH THE FAILINGS OF THE WEAK AND NOT TO PLEASE OURSELVES. EACH OF US SHOULD PLEASE HIS NEIGHBOR FOR HIS GOOD, TO BUILD HIM UP. FOR EVEN CHRIST DID NOT PLEASE HIMSELF …FOR EVERYTHING THAT WAS WRITTEN IN THE PAST WAS WRITTEN TO TEACH US, SO THAT *THROUGH ENDURANCE AND THE ENCOURAGEMENT OF THE SCRIPTURES WE MIGHT HAVE HOPE*. MAY THE GOD WHO GIVES ENDURANCE AND ENCOURAGEMENT GIVE YOU A SPIRIT OF UNITY AMONG YOURSELVES AS YOU FOLLOW CHRIST JESUS, SO THAT WITH ONE HEART AND MOUTH YOU MAY GLORIFY THE GOD AND FATHER OF OUR LORD JESUS CHRIST. ACCEPT ONE ANOTHER, THEN, JUST AS CHRIST ACCEPTED YOU, IN ORDER TO BRING PRAISE TO GOD. *[Romans 15:1–7]*

ENGAGE

1. **KEY** What was your family of origin like when it came to building a sense of hope in you? Check all that apply; even contradictory statements may have been true of your family. Share with the group as much as you feel comfortable.

   - ❑ My family always built up my sense of hope
   - ❑ My family situation drained my hope at times
   - ❑ It was neutral — I was sort of left to find my own hope.
   - ❑ I really learned a lot about building others up from my family (explain...)
   - ❑ I felt torn down a lot by my family
   - ❑ Other: ____

2. Answer these questions about yourself:
   In my most important relationships, do I tend to be an encourager or a critic? A cheerleader or a dream-killer?

3. Would people with whom I am in relationships agree with my answers to that question?

4. Why do you think that is, and how does it compare with who you'd like to be?

5. **KEY** René talked about *"letting the Word of Christ dwell in me richly" [Colossians 3:16]*. This means to let the truths from God's Word really take root in my soul. Let's consider the truths from the first few weeks; glance back over your notes from sessions 1 through 3 and then answer the following questions.

   - How does really believing the promises of God, the truths about God, and the truths about my identity in Christ enable me to truly bless others — and not just be superficially nice?

   - Read Ephesians 4:29 out loud. Practically speaking, what should not come out of our mouths? What types of things should we say? Why can this be so hard to do?

   - Read Romans 15:1–7 out loud. How could this help you re-frame relationships in your life?

APPLY

Exercises

1. **KEY** Practice spreading hope today through this exercise: Choose one person in your group to receive encouraging, positive, hope-building statements from everyone else in the group (e.g., "I have noticed that you are really good at..." or "This week you were a good example to me by..."). Then go clockwise to the next person in the group until each person has had a chance to be encouraged by the group's statements.

2. **KEY** Take some time to individually fill in the blanks below with ideas about how you can spread hope to four specific people or groups in your life. Perhaps through a card, a letter, a phone call, a compliment, an act of service, a specific observation about a strength, or an offer to study Scripture — everyone needs hope! How will you spread hope this week?

   The way I see myself building hope in the life of ____________________
   this week is to ____

   The way I see myself building hope in the life of ____________________
   this week is to ____

   The way I see myself building hope in the life of ____________________
   this week is to ____

   The way I see myself building hope in the life of ____________________
   this week is to ____

Now share some of your ideas with your group. And next week, share what happened when you followed through on these ideas!

GROUP PROJECTS

One great way to share hope with others is to contribute to a local food pantry. Most of us have little idea how hopeless people can feel when they don't even have enough food for their family. Food pantries don't just feed people physically; they really are an encouragement to their spirits.

So consider making these next two weeks your food drive weeks, as a group project! Collect food and either individually bring it to church, or collect it at the next two group meetings and bring it in together. This week, pray about your individual and group goals for the food drive!

If you have extra cards, write some more notes of affirmation today to people you think could use a dose of hope. (One idea: Work off the church prayer list.)

PRAYER

Ask your group to pray for you in specific ways as you set out to build hope in others this week.

Share your other prayer requests with your small group and then take time to pray together.

BEFORE YOU LEAVE

Take a few minutes to talk about where and when you will meet next week, and who will be in charge of any meals or snacks.

WEEK 5

LIVING WITH HOPE DAILY

Be joyful in hope, patient in affliction, faithful in prayer.

[Romans 12:12]

DAY

29

SUNDAY

by René Schlaepfer

Expecting the Best

> "You answer us with awesome deeds of righteousness, O God our Savior, the hope of all the ends of the earth and of the farthest seas." *[Psalm 65:5]*

In his book *Windows of Hope*, Richard Lee tells the true story of famous Navy Admiral James Stockdale. One of the first POWs of the Vietnam War, Stockdale was frequently tortured during his seven years in a prison camp. After his release, Stockdale said **the only thing that kept him alive was hope**: Hope with each new day that he might be released before sundown. He knew that without this sense of **daily anticipation** he would have died, like so many others without hope.

What was good for Stockdale is good for you! **Do you have daily anticipation that God will show up in your life and open doors for you?** Do you anticipate the "awesome deeds" the psalmist writes about in today's verse?

One important reminder: Our culture uses the word *hope* almost interchangeably with the word *wish* ("I hope I win the lottery!"). But the Bible defines hope differently: As a confident expectation that God will keep the promises in His Word.

The Bible promises…

- The hope of the resurrection *[1 Corinthians 15:20–23]*
- The hope of our glorification *[Galatians 5:5]*
- The hope of eternal life *[1 Corinthians 9:25; 1 John 2:17]*
- The hope of deliverance *[Psalm 33:16–18]*
- The hope of salvation *[Ephesians 1:13–14]*
- The hope of the Second Coming of Christ *[1 Thessalonians 4:13–14]*
- The hope that in all things God will work for the good *[Romans 8:28]*

As Lee points out, substitute the word *assurance* or *conviction* for hope in the list above, and you start to get the biblical idea of hope! This week we'll emphasize the sense of expectation that hope-filled people can live with each day!

Do I live with daily anticipation that God will act in my life? What difference would this make in my conversations, my relationships, my work?

PRAYER

Heavenly Father, help me have hope as I start each day that You will act in a powerful way!

ACTION

This week, spread hope to others by participating in a food drive or other community service project!

Living with Daily Expectation

DAY
30
MONDAY
by René Schlaepfer

This is the day the Lord has made; Let us rejoice and be glad in it! *[Psalm 118:24]*

Because I was raised by Swiss parents in a Silicon Valley suburb I enjoyed many European holiday traditions that, at least in my childhood, were unfamiliar to my American friends. One of my favorites: Advent calendars! Each day in December I would anticipate opening another little door. At first I'd look forward to simply seeing a new picture; eventually advent calendars hid chocolates or even little toys! It spread out the Christmas joy; the thrill of opening a present touched every day, not just December 25th.

That's a lot like living with biblical hope! It fills you with expectation, not just of the ultimate Day when all your hopes will be fulfilled, but of the way God will work each day until then.

Try this experiment: As soon you wake up each day for the rest of the Hope Experience, say to yourself, "This is the day the Lord has made; I **will** rejoice and be glad in it!" I've been trying this for a few months and it has really changed my outlook; it reminds me each day is sort of like a little advent calendar door, with something God wants me to experience inside — an opportunity to serve, to grow, to laugh. I can miss it if I'm not looking.

Yet advent calendars simply wouldn't work without the big double doors labeled "December 25." Anticipating that day was exactly what made the other, smaller advent doors so magical for me as a kid. Again, much like biblical hope. That daily sense of expectation is made more wondrous as you anticipate the Great Day — the day of your resurrection and God's glorious re-creation of the heavens and earth. You want to spread not just Christmas cheer, but "resurrection cheer."

C. S. Lewis pointed out this link:

> Hope means a continual looking forward to the eternal world. It does not mean that we are to leave the present world as it is. If you read history you will find that the Christians who did the most for the present world were just those who thought most of the next… It is since Christians have largely ceased to think of the other world that they have become so ineffective in this. Aim at Heaven and you will get earth 'thrown in'; aim at earth and you will get neither.

How can I remind myself to live each day in hopeful expectation?

PRAYER

Lord, I choose to rejoice in this day. I know there will be "advent calendar doors" for me to open today, that You place in my life. Help me live with a daily hopefulness and expectation.

DAY

31

TUESDAY

by Kim Breuninger

The Suspense is Part of the Fun

I WAIT FOR THE LORD, MY SOUL WAITS, AND IN HIS WORD I PUT MY HOPE. *[Psalm 130:5]*

✹ ***Read Psalm 130***

There's a scene in *Charlie and the Chocolate Factory* where Willie Wonka says, "The suspense is terrible. I hope it will last!"

I'm with him! I love the tension between hoping... and waiting... and then finally knowing. We may as well learn to love the suspense, because it's a daily part of life.

Imagine yourself standing in line at a scary roller coaster you're about to ride. Talking and laughing with your friends, you try to act nonchalant but really you're shaking inside and semi-seriously considering the "chicken exit." The suspense is intense, but for a roller-coaster fan it's also half the fun!

Now apply that to the roller coaster of life. There will always be tension between the *now* and the *not yet*. But that does not have to turn into debilitating anxiety. The very act of waiting is itself part of the experience that God wants you to learn from... and even enjoy.

But only if you wait in *hope* instead of *worry*. Ask yourself this question: *"Am I suffering more in my worries than in my actual circumstances?"* If so, then you may have a bad case of a lack of hope!

For many of us, our limited knowledge of the future creates fear. Of course, we experience limited knowledge every day so we could always find reasons to fear. For one thing, our knowledge of God is limited, so we wonder, "Will He answer my prayers the way I want Him to?" "Does He see my suffering?" "Will I be okay?"

Thankfully we have a God who promises that although our life's journey is unpredictable we can trust in Him through every dip, dive and turn. We needn't suffer because of an unknown hope and an unknown future. Christ died and rose again in order to become our living hope. And it's because of His promise of unfailing love that we can live through any of life's circumstances or delays with great expectation!

What are my emotions as I daily "wait in line" in my life? On which do I rely more, my limited knowledge of God or His unlimited power and love?

PRAYER

Father, sometimes I get impatient and take matters into my own hands instead of trusting in You. Sometimes I doubt Your involvement or concern over the details of my life. Lord, help me to remember that You love me so much that You created me in Your image and for Your glory and that You will let nothing separate us.

Joyful in Hope

by Dave Hicks

> BE JOYFUL IN HOPE, PATIENT IN AFFLICTION, FAITHFUL IN PRAYER.
> *{Romans 12:12}*

Read Romans 12:9–13

The way it's used by many today, the word "hope" can imply a frustrated, lonely longing: "I hope I meet someone." "I hope I get married." "I hope I have children." The idea of being *"joyful in hope"* may seem unusual.

But the "hope" we're talking about during these weeks is NOT about unrealistic expectations...naive dreaming...or wishful thinking. IT IS a joyful, quiet confidence in a reality that is not yet.

It's like the mid-December afternoon when I was 8 years old. I was digging through the back recesses of our basement in Altadena and came upon a brand new blue bicycle...just my size. I realized I must have stumbled across a future Christmas present. It was something I had said I wanted but had been told was not possible because of my brother's medical bills.

I kept my discovery a secret, but there was a quiet joy in my life during the next couple weeks. I was more patient with my sick brother. I found myself striking up conversations with my father. There still was no bike... I still had to watch my friends ride their bikes past my house each day... I still walked to school. But there was a joyful hope that had entered my life. Once I saw my father's sacrifice for me in the middle of our family's hardship and suffering, a patience and peace came over me. It replaced my detachment and self-pity.

In the same way spiritually, once I catch a glimpse of God's great love for me, His personal suffering and willing sacrifice, I become a changed person; one who is *"joyful in hope"* and surprisingly *"patient in affliction,"* whatever that might be, every day!

My family always opened all our presents together on Christmas Eve. I finished opening the usual pajamas, annual sweater, and socks from Aunt Erma. Still no bike! But I climbed into bed that Christmas Eve, in my new pajamas, with *"joyful hope"*: A trust that **what is not yet...WILL BE!!!**

How can I live with "joyful hope" ...today?

PRAYER

Lord, help me to find joy in hope today.

DAY
33
THURSDAY
by René Schlaepfer

Beyond Pessimism and Optimism

...A FAITH AND KNOWLEDGE RESTING ON THE HOPE OF ETERNAL LIFE, WHICH GOD, WHO DOES NOT LIE, PROMISED BEFORE THE BEGINNING OF TIME. *[Titus 1:2]*

✹ *Read Titus 1:1–3*

During his time as a prisoner of the Nazis, German pastor Dietrich Bonhoeffer wrote to a friend that he was neither a pessimist (expecting things to get worse) nor an optimist (expecting things to get better). He said that he was **living by hope**.

What's the difference? Pessimists doubt anything good will happen. Optimists believe only good will happen. But a hopeful person is realistic: He acknowledges there may be immediate suffering — but ultimate reward.

Bonhoeffer knew what the early Christians knew: As long as I am alive, even in prison, God will use whatever happens to me for good (it happened for Bonhoeffer — his prison letters still inspire readers today); and even if I die, I am promised heaven... and the resurrection! When everything was stripped away from him, this hope is what remained, and what sustained him on a daily basis.

In today's verses from Titus 1:1–3, Paul reminds Titus that **our entire faith rests on hope**; specifically the hope of eternal life God promised to us. It is the only thing that cannot be taken away from us, even in prison. This is sometimes forgotten by Christians who try to make their hope rest on other foundations.

Writing during the 2008 economic meltdown, Gordon MacDonald said:

> God intends that Christians ask once again: **"What is at the core of the real gospel that we may have forgotten during the days of prosperity?"** May hopeful people relearn how to differentiate between the "city" of today and the enduring city that is to come. Such hope — liberally spread — could have revival proportions.

I agree. Do an honest self-evaluation: Does my faith rest solidly on the hope of eternal life?

Am I a pessimist, an optimist, or am I living by hope? How can I live by hope in my expectations today?

PRAYER

Lord, help me today to live not as a pessimist or a blind optimist, but as a biblically optimistic, hopeful person!

DAY
34
FRIDAY
by René Schlaepfer

Living Hope that Never Fades

PRAISE BE TO THE GOD AND FATHER OF OUR LORD JESUS CHRIST! IN HIS GREAT MERCY HE HAS GIVEN US NEW BIRTH INTO A LIVING HOPE THROUGH THE RESURRECTION OF JESUS CHRIST FROM THE DEAD.
[1 Peter 1:3]

Read 1 Peter 1:3–9

I often hear Christians fretting about the latest headlines.

With each new crisis, many seem to worry: "Is this Armageddon?" "Is it the end of America as we know it?" "Are we in the last days?"

Well, think about this: For many of the first century believers, it *was* the end of their lives as they knew it. And they sincerely believed they *were* living in the last days. Yet when you read their letters in the New Testament, what do you see?

G. Campbell Morgan was a great Scottish preacher in the time of World War II. Imagine hearing him say these words in his Scottish brogue:

> I have no sympathy with those who tell us these are the darkest days this world has ever seen! The days in which we live *are* appalling. But they don't compare to the days of the first Christians. Notwithstanding, the dominant tone of their letters is one of triumph; in fact, we never see them cast down, we never see them suffering from pessimism fever, they're always triumphant! If ever I am tempted to think that religion is dead today, it is when I listen to the wailing of some Christian people, "Everything is going wrong!" Oh, be quiet! Think again! Judge again! **Not by the circumstances of this passing hour, but by the infinite things of our gospel and our God!** That is exactly what the writers of this New Testament did!

I love that. Reread 1 Peter 1:3–9 for an example of this. The readers were suffering *"in all kinds of trials,"* yet Peter tells them they have a *"living hope"* that can never fade.

Do not stake your happiness on circumstances, which can change so quickly, but on the infinite hope promised you by your God!

What circumstances are creating anxiety in my life? How does trust in my living hope, my unchanging inheritance, give me serenity today?

PRAYER

Lord, help me to be soaked to my soul with a sense of hope, and with the peace that passes all understanding. I get nervous, and I need You to calm me down with the peace of Christ.

DAY
35
SATURDAY
by Valerie Webb

Hope in the Midst of Trouble

WE ALSO REJOICE IN OUR SUFFERINGS, BECAUSE WE KNOW THAT SUFFERING PRODUCES PERSEVERANCE; PERSEVERANCE, CHARACTER; AND CHARACTER, HOPE. *[Romans 5:3b–4]*

Read Romans 5:1–11

I think we all long to be hopeful, people of hope. This passage, however, tells us that hope shines brightest in suffering. I want hope, but I sure don't want trouble!

Verses 3 and 4 lead us through the path that suffering can take in our character and emotions. Now it doesn't have to take this path. We can choose other paths: control, anger, bitterness, cynicism. But none of these paths end in hope.

Paul says that our suffering can ultimately produce hope. I, for one, love knowing that my troubles are not in vain. I know not all suffering has an earthly explanation, but it is great to know **suffering has a path, and that path ends with a growing hope!**

But don't stop there; verse 5 has to be one of the best verses in the Bible! *"And hope does not disappoint us, because God has poured out his love..."* Once again we see the Bible does not talk about hope for hope's sake; that would be a hope that disappoints. The Bible directs us to hope in God.

I am struck by reading the phrase, *"And hope does not disappoint us, because* G*OD...*" What hope, what joy, what peace there is "*...because* G*OD...*" What more do we need to know when it comes to hope?

Meditate on the phrase, "And hope does not disappoint us, because God...." How can that impact my response to life's ups and downs?

PRAYER

Lord, I choose to put my hope in Your promise that suffering can produce positive effects in my life.

Small Group Lesson 5

WEEK
5
SMALL GROUP

Am I a Yesterday Person or a Tomorrow Person?

LEADER'S NOTE Please review these questions before beginning in order to select those that will be most meaningful and effective for your group. Do not feel obligated to answer them all. But please try and discuss at least one from each section especially the **KEY** questions. Make sure you allow adequate time for prayer and to discuss the next group assignment.

CONNECT

1. **KEY** What caught your attention, challenged or encouraged you in the weekend message or the devotionals?

2. How has focusing on hope over the past five weeks helped you?

WATCH THE VIDEO

❋ Biblically founded hope changes my expectations about the future

1. Hope changes the way I see ________________________________

   For if, when we were God's enemies, we were reconciled to him through the death of his Son, how much more, having been reconciled, shall we be saved through his life!
   [Romans 5:10]

2. Hope changes the way I see ________________________________

   - God is ultimately in control *[2 Chronicles 29:8]*
   - God will be my refuge in every trial *[Psalm 50:15, 59:16]*
   - There is promised spiritual benefit from every trial *[Romans 8:28]*
   - There is a promise of future reward for every trial I endure *[2 Corinthians 4:16–17]*

Therefore we do not lose heart. Though outwardly we are wasting away, yet inwardly we are being renewed day by day. For our light and momentary troubles are achieving for us an eternal glory that far outweighs them all. *[2 Corinthians 4:16–17]*

3. Hope changes the way I see ____________________________

• God has given me weapons to defend against the enemy's attack *[Ephesians 6:10–18]*

• I do not have to sin *[Romans 8:2–4]*

• God does not condemn me if I am in Christ:

Therefore, there is now no condemnation for those who are in Christ Jesus. *[Romans 8:1]*

4. Hope changes the way I see ____________________________

For we are God's workmanship, created in Christ Jesus to do good works, which God prepared in advance for us to do. *[Ephesians 2:10]*

5. Hope changes the way I see ____________________________

• Death has been swallowed up in victory *[1 Corinthians 15:56–57]*

• Because Jesus was resurrected, those in Christ will be resurrected too *[1 Corinthians 15:20]*

• Not even death can separate me from God's love *[Romans 8:38–39]*

• Death is a beginning, not just an end:

For I am already being poured out like a drink offering, and the time has come for my departure. I have fought the good fight, I have finished the race, I have kept the faith. Now there is in store for me the crown of righteousness, which the Lord, the righteous Judge, will award to me on that day—and not only to me, but also to all who have longed for his appearing. *[2 Timothy 4:6–8]*

List adapted from Nathan Busenitz' "Living a Life of Hope"

WEEK 5 SMALL GROUP

ENGAGE

1. **KEY** Do you tend to have positive or negative expectations of the future?

   - ❏ I am always waiting for the other shoe to drop
   - ❏ Even when things go well, I suspect soon things will go wrong again — like they usually do for me
   - ❏ I fear the unexpected
   - ❏ I am afraid of losing control
   - ❏ I worry about making poor decisions that will impact my future
   - ❏ Other:

✹ Review the video notes

2. When you face a difficult situation, in which of the five areas do you struggle with being a "yesterday person," doubting God's truths?

3. In which of the 5 areas is it easier for you to be a tomorrow person, filled with hope and positive expectations of the future? How have theses verses (or others) shaped these positive expectations?

4. **KEY** Read 2 Corinthians 4:7–5:7 out loud in your group. You may not immediately understand every one of Paul's poetic phrases, but what do you think is his main point in these verses about how he is responding to his current suffering and what he believes about his future?

5. What kind of life is described in verses 4:8–9?

6. Are these kinds of life experiences any different for the Christian or the non-Christian?

7. **KEY** Even though Paul has been through all these experiences, what does he say in these verses to show that he is a tomorrow person, clearly looking forward to the future with eagerness?

8. What does it mean to "walk by faith and not by sight"?

9. How do these verses make you feel about hard times?

WEEK

5

SMALL GROUP

APPLY

1. KEY If Sarah Winchester had come to you and asked for help, what would you have said to her, based on what you have learned so far in the Hope experience? Keep in mind that she was apparently obsessed with questions like, "Why have I suffered so much? What must I do to absolve myself from my guilt? Is there future hope and security for me?"

2. By believing the promises of God you are enabled to have an ultimately positive expectation about the future. How have you found that true in your life?

3. What steps will you take this week to be a **tomorrow person** instead of a **yesterday person**?

PRAYER

KEY How can we as a group pray for you this week?

BEFORE YOU LEAVE

Take a few minutes to talk about where and when you will meet next week, and who will be in charge of any meals or snacks.

WEEK 6
HOPE WHEN LIFE SEEMS HOPELESS

Why are you in despair, O my soul? ...Hope in God...
[Psalm 42:11 NASB]

DAY
36
SUNDAY
by René Schlaepfer

When Hope is Shattered

Against all hope, Abraham in hope believed...
[Romans 4:18a]

Read Romans 4:17–22

The famous Christian writer and thinker G. K. Chesterton said:

> Hope means hoping when things are hopeless, or it is no virtue at all... As long as matters are really hopeful, hope is mere flattery or platitude; **it is only when everything is hopeless that hope begins to be a strength.**

This week let's focus on hope in the midst of suffering and shattered dreams. In today's passage the Apostle Paul recounts the story of Abraham. God had promised that one day Abraham would be the father of many people, but at age ninety-nine, Abraham still didn't have any children, and his wife Sarah had been infertile her whole life. It was an impossible situation.

Maybe you can relate. Perhaps you're feeling pretty hopeless in some area of your own life. You wonder: Where do I put my hope now?

Where did Abraham put his hope? Himself? No. His feelings? No. Positive thinking? No. He believed in God's *promise* to him.

See, **positive thinking and hope are not the same thing**. Positive thinking helps a lot — in situations where you have control over the outcome. But positive thinking is worth little when things are out of your control. Only hope in God's promises helps then.

Of course, God never promises He will do things the way you expect, according to your timetable. That certainly didn't happen for Abraham and Sarah! But God promises He'll keep His word. And He promises it's when things are hopeless that I'll grow in ways I never could have imagined!

Eventually Abraham and Sarah had a miracle baby. And they named him Isaac, which means "laughter," because they had laughed at the promise of a child. But, as they say, God always has the last laugh!

Where do I feel hopeless in my life right now? What promises of God can I cling to for hope?

PRAYER

Lord, I confess to You an area where I feel little hope today. I claim Your specific promises that You will mold me into the image of Christ, that You will "birth" a new person in me!

When God Seems Silent

Why are you in despair, O my soul? ...Hope in God...
[Psalm 42:11 NASB]

by Paul Spurlock

✸ ***Read Psalm 42***

Seeing people talk loudly to themselves in public is quite common today — usually they're on a cell phone with a wireless earpiece. But before the Bluetooth era, speaking out loud to yourself in public made most observers wonder about your sanity!

Well, I once was just such a talker. I was going through an intense depression that lasted a couple of *years*. Feeling ignored by God — no, abandoned — I used to walk alone for hours in a large park, talking audibly to God through angry tears. I'd even curse at Him, all the while shaking my fist toward the heavens and crying: *"I'd rather have Your discipline than Your silence, for at least in the discipline I'd have Your presence!"* But still, I experienced only silence (and odd looks from passersby!). It seemed God was nowhere to be found.

It's hard for people who've never experienced the blackness of depression to relate, but apparently the writer of Psalm 42 felt the same way. He cries out: *"Tears have been my food day and night while men say to me all day long, 'Where is your God?'"* A few verses later he sums up his sad state — his soul is "downcast" and "disturbed."

How did the psalmist recover? Interestingly, he describes himself as a thirsty *"deer" [v. 1]* — instead of a more self-sufficient animal like a camel. I think this is a clue — **choose to rely on God instead your own resources.** Next, in verse 4, he draws strength by recalling the *"joy"* of being in the *"house of God."* **So when down, seek the people of God!** Then, despite "downcast" circumstances, he doesn't forget to "praise" God *[v. 5]*. Finally, he sums it up all in one phrase: *"put your hope in God"*! Is he merely a naïve Pollyanna? No. The psalmist's focus — and foundation for **real** hope — is clearly beyond the here and now. Proclaiming that his hope is set upon the *"rock" [v. 9]*, and *"Savior...God" [v. 11]* is a focus on eternal concerns. In this he found true hope!

I eventually came out of my three-year desert of having no sense of God's presence. It came to me as it did the psalmist, through putting my hope in God, no matter what the circumstances. Like a broken bone now healed, my relationship to God is stronger — and more hopeful — as a result!

When have I felt like God was silent? How can hope impact those times of silence?

PRAYER

Lord, I want real hope! Help me get beyond the here and now—and put my hope in the only One who can save me now and for all eternity!

DAY
38
TUESDAY
by Hannah Deutsch

Hope in the Dark

FOR IN THIS HOPE WE WERE SAVED. BUT HOPE THAT IS SEEN IS NO HOPE AT ALL. WHO HOPES FOR WHAT HE ALREADY HAS?
[Romans 8:24]

Read Romans 8:18–25

Have you ever been afraid of drowning? Most of us would probably say yes. It's a pretty common fear, right?

But I'm not talking about a fear of drowning in water. I used to feel like I was drowning in the middle of the grocery store, in the park on a sunny afternoon, sometimes in my own living room.

I had just given birth to our second baby about a month before, and by that fourth or fifth postpartum week, I was drowning in depression. I would sometimes literally raise my arms up in hopes that God would reach down and pull me out of the depths of my despair. I had never experienced such a deep, dark, hopeless depression like this, and most days my thoughts were so scattered I felt like I couldn't even pray!

So, I began to pray like this: "Help! Help! Help!" and I knew God knew the rest. I started to get more and more desperate for a way out, something to help me get through the long, tearful, anxiety-ridden days, something to help me to be able to care for my husband and two older children even though I felt like a total wreck, inside and out. But through all that time as I cried out to God, over and over again I heard one simple phrase whispered back to me: "I will heal you." I wanted to shout, "When? How? Why do I have to be in this place any longer? Why won't you just heal me right now, Lord? WHY?"

Looking back I can see now that He was healing me, slowly but surely. Only God knows why we have to go through those times and only He can use them for good. He taught me many things through that difficult time when things were so dark I felt like I couldn't see my hand in front of my face. He taught me that my husband will love me and stand by me no matter what. He taught me that it's okay to let my children see me weep and be imperfect and needy for the Lord. He taught me that it's okay to accept the help, kindness and charity from other believers. But most of all, He taught me to hope in Him and that He will ALWAYS be there with me, even in the darkest of times.

Recall a dark time where I wondered why God allowed it to happen. What did He teach me during that time? If I feel I'm waiting on God to deliver me through a hard time right now, have I asked Him for help and healing?

PRAYER

Lord, thank You so much for being with me always, in good times and hard times. Thank You for being more than worthy of my trust and hope and for loving me and healing me.

Prisoners of Hope

✹ *Read Zechariah 9:9–12*

by Mark Spurlock

> "Mama, I am tired, tired of suffering. These years of captivity have shown me that I am not as resistant, nor as brave, intelligent or strong as I had believed. I have tried to maintain hope, as one keeps one's head above water."

Ingrid Betancourt penned these words somewhere in the jungles of Colombia—held hostage by a rebel militia for six years. Her health was failing, and so was her hope.

Then, on July 3, 2008, Ingrid and 14 other hostages were rescued in a daring military operation that succeeded without firing a single shot! Images of Ingrid's joyous homecoming were plastered on TVs and newspapers around the world. Few things are more stirring than seeing captives set free and families reunited!

The "prisoners of hope" to whom Zechariah wrote were Israelites living in exile — captives of Babylon for 70 years. With each passing year they must have asked, "Where is God? When will He save us? Is there any hope for us?"

Maybe you've asked similar questions. Is there any hope for me? Imprisonment needn't involve chains, guards or a foreign army. It could be a habit or attitude — a stubborn sin that's taken you captive. Maybe it's loneliness. Perhaps you're not as resistant, or strong as you had believed. I know I'm not. So what do we do when we feel the weight of our bonds? Zechariah says, *"Return to your fortress, O prisoners of hope..."* *[Zechariah 9:12]*

Who is our fortress? Today's verses tell us that, too: *"See, your king comes to you, righteous and having salvation, gentle and riding on a donkey..."* *[Zechariah 9:9]* Hmm...remind you of anyone? *[See Matthew 21:1–9]*.

Why not take a moment to return to your fortress right now? The familiar hymn, *Turn Your Eyes Upon Jesus*, begins like this...

> *O soul, are you weary and troubled? No light in the darkness you see?*
> *There's a light for a look at the Savior, And life more abundant and free!*

If you know the chorus, take a moment to hum or sing the song as you fix your focus on the One who sets us free and renews our hope!

Where in my life do I feel in bondage? How does Jesus set me free? Reaffirm Christ's victory and power over whatever is causing you to feel like a prisoner of hope!

PRAYER

Lord, help me return to the fortress of love and hope found in You.

DAY
40
THURSDAY
by Mark Spurlock

Write down a time in your life when you felt hopeless. What do you know now that you didn't know then? What is sapping your hope now? What do you know about God that can renew your hope today?

PRAYER

Lord, please renew my hope today. Help me to take encouragement from the fact that You are my reason to hope.

Wait until the End of the Story

Read Ruth 1:8–13 & 4:14–17

> EVEN IF I THOUGHT THERE WAS STILL HOPE FOR ME...THE LORD'S HAND HAS GONE OUT AGAINST ME! *[Ruth 1:12–13]*

Naomi spoke these words when she couldn't envision anything but a miserable future. Having lost her husband — and then her two sons — she loses hope in God as well.

Just how essential is hope?

I came across a fascinating story about the town of Flagstaff, Maine. In the 1940s demand for hydroelectric power was so great the state decided to redirect a river into the valley where Flagstaff stood for 100 years. Flagstaff was a picturesque New England village with lovingly maintained homes and shops. But as soon as word spread about the town being flooded, all repairs stopped. What's the use of painting a house that's going to end up under water? Week by week the whole town became more bedraggled — broken windows, littered streets, overgrown yards. Flagstaff didn't die when the waters came. Flagstaff died the day it lost hope.

That's why it's so important to keep renewing your hope, whether it's in your relationship with God or another person. When does any relationship become neglected? When there's no hope! The weeds set in, the paint starts to peel, and eventually we think: "There's nothing here worth saving."

Naomi said as much. **But like we often do, Naomi speaks before knowing how the story ends!** And when God blesses her with a new family and future through her daughter-in-law Ruth, Naomi's bitterness is replaced by joy! With Naomi doting on her new grandson, her friends say, *"Praise be to the Lord...He will renew your life and sustain you in your old age." [Ruth 4:14–15]*

Remember Naomi the next time you feel like you've lost hope. You may not know what God has in store — but He does! And because God is in your future, you always have a reason to hope.

Motivated by Hope

by René Schlaepfer

> Now faith is being sure of what we hope for and certain of what we do not see. This is what the ancients were commended for. *[Hebrews 11:1–2]*

In yesterday's reading Mark Spurlock told the true story of Flagstaff, Maine. When that town fell into disrepair many years before the dam upriver was finished, someone asked, "Why?" The answer famously came back: **"If there is no hope in the future, there is no motivation in the present."**

Victor Frankl, a Jewish psychologist, discovered this truth in a Nazi concentration camp during World War II. Frankl began observing fellow prisoners to discover what coping mechanism could help him endure. Here's what he found: People who could not make their present suffering fit with their faith, who could not find its meaning in their world view, despaired and eventually gave up and died. But those who could find meaning from their faith were then able to find hope for a future beyond their present suffering, and they survived!

The writer of the book of Hebrews reminds his readers of this very truth in Hebrews chapter 11. Writing to Christians who were tempted to give up on their faith because of persecution, he paints a stirring picture of the ancient heroes of the faith who braved dangers, endured suffering, and took huge risks because they had something to live — and die — for: The promise of God that the best was yet to come. He says that this is the very essence of faith. Then he challenges his readers to have the same kind of endurance based on faith and hope.

Read Hebrews 11:32–40. What future hope prompted these believers to continue to have hope and faith even when God didn't seem to "come through" for them?

How does hope in the future provide motivation in the present? How do you see this truth in the world around you? If you were in a prison like the one Victor Frankl survived, how would your faith, your world view, help you deal with your suffering?

PRAYER

Lord, help my hope in the future give me motivation in the present!

DAY

42

SATURDAY

by Kelly Welty

How do I typically respond when I feel under attack? Do my responses show fear or hope?

PRAYER

Lord, help me not to be surprised when mere humans let me down. Help me remember that ultimately, my only true hope is You.

ACTION

Remember to contribute to this week's "Spread Hope Project": the wrap-up of a food drive! This brings hope in a tangible way to those who need it badly!

Hope When I Am Attacked

...You are God my Savior, and my hope is in you all day long. *[Psalm 25:5b]*

Read Psalm 25:1–7

Cathy (not her real name) was a co-worker and friend at a local photo lab. In the same week we had both been transferred from a smaller satellite operation to the Main Lab — sort of like being called up from the Minors to the Big Leagues. It was a very stress-filled and demanding transition for me, so I was especially bothered to hear rumors of how Cathy was talking about me to other coworkers. Many second-hand accounts of her rants reached me and I was at a loss to explain them.

A few weeks went by and I finally had a chance to ask her privately what I had done to offend her. She started crying. She admitted she was bashing me so she'd look more competent and would keep her job if either of us were deemed redundant. Her husband was out of work, they were struggling financially, and her fear had caused her to make up lies about me. I knew there had to be a story behind it, but I still felt the sting of the attack.

In this psalm, King David is enduring one of the many low points of his rule and his enemies choose that very moment to attack. They not only test the strength of his borders but the quality of his character. They make up stories and false accusations in an attempt to ruin him both physically and emotionally. Here he pleads with God to save his life and reputation. He's honest enough to admit he's blown it in the past, but in this recent attack he can find no reason for his suffering. His heart turns to the One who has been unchanging, the single constant in his life. He longs to understand God's ways and he places his trust in the consistency of His truth.

David knows he can't change the way his enemies treat him or the circumstances of his life, but his one Hope is in the unwavering mercy and love of God for His children.

We see such a small piece of the picture, it's no wonder we don't understand what's happening in our lives. Our only hope is to trust the One who sees and knows all.

WEEK 6 SMALL GROUP

Small Group Lesson 6

Finding Hope When My Hope is Shattered

LEADER'S NOTE Please review these questions before beginning in order to select those that will be most meaningful and effective for your group. Do not feel obligated to answer them all. But please try to discuss at least one from each section, especially the **KEY** questions, allowing adequate time for prayer and to discuss the group assignment.

CONNECT

1. **KEY** What caught your attention, challenged or encouraged you in the weekend message or the devotionals?

2. Who do you admire for facing shattered dreams and yet remaining hopeful? How do you think they maintain this hopeful attitude?

WATCH THE VIDEO

God wants to rebuild lives and restore shattered hopes

> Then I said to them, "You see the trouble we are in: Jerusalem lies in ruins, and its gates have been burned with fire. *Come, let us rebuild the wall* of Jerusalem, and we will no longer be in disgrace." I also told them about the gracious hand of my God upon me and what the king had said to me. They replied, "Let us start rebuilding." So they began this good work. *[Nehemiah 2:17–18]*

Hope is not something I generate myself. It happens as I focus on who God is, how He perceives me, and what He promises about the present and the future. All through the Bible, God speaks words of hope to people who have suffered the deaths of loved ones, persecution, war, and other trials...

> "Moses my servant is dead. Now then, you and all these people, get ready to cross the Jordan River into the land I am about to give to them — to the Israelites... As I was with Moses, so I will be with you; I will never leave you

NOR FORSAKE YOU. BE STRONG AND COURAGEOUS, BECAUSE YOU WILL LEAD THESE PEOPLE TO INHERIT THE LAND I SWORE TO THEIR FOREFATHERS TO GIVE THEM. BE STRONG AND VERY COURAGEOUS… HAVE I NOT COMMANDED YOU? BE STRONG AND COURAGEOUS. DO NOT BE TERRIFIED; DO NOT BE DISCOURAGED, FOR THE LORD YOUR GOD WILL BE WITH YOU WHEREVER YOU GO." *[Joshua 1:2–9]*

NO EYE HAS SEEN, NO EAR HAS HEARD, NO MIND HAS CONCEIVED WHAT GOD HAS PREPARED FOR THOSE WHO LOVE HIM. *[1 Corinthians 2:9b]*

"CALL TO ME AND I WILL ANSWER YOU AND TELL YOU GREAT AND UNSEARCHABLE THINGS YOU DO NOT KNOW." *[Jeremiah 33:3]*

Attitudes For Survival

List adapted from H. Norman Wright's "Tomorrow Can Be Different". Verses added by TLC staff.

"I will examine God's promises and let them guide what I do in the present."

MY SOUL FAINTS WITH LONGING FOR YOUR SALVATION, BUT *I HAVE PUT MY HOPE IN YOUR WORD.* *[Psalm 119:81]*

I WAIT FOR THE LORD, MY SOUL WAITS, AND *IN HIS WORD I PUT MY HOPE.* *[Psalm 130:5]*

"No matter what happens, I will not be defeated."

NO, IN ALL THESE THINGS *WE ARE MORE THAN CONQUERORS* THROUGH HIM WHO LOVED US. *[Romans 8:37]*

"I am a blessed person regardless of what I have experienced."

PRAISE BE TO THE GOD AND FATHER OF OUR LORD JESUS CHRIST, WHO *HAS BLESSED US* IN THE HEAVENLY REALMS WITH *EVERY SPIRITUAL BLESSING* IN CHRIST. *[Ephesians 1:3]*

"I can find meaning in situations that involve suffering or great loss."

AND WE KNOW THAT *IN ALL THINGS* GOD WORKS FOR THE GOOD OF THOSE WHO LOVE HIM, WHO HAVE BEEN CALLED ACCORDING TO HIS PURPOSE. *[Romans 8:28]*

IF WE ARE DISTRESSED, IT IS FOR YOUR COMFORT AND SALVATION;

IF WE ARE COMFORTED, IT IS FOR YOUR COMFORT, WHICH PRODUCES IN YOU PATIENT ENDURANCE OF THE SAME SUFFERINGS WE SUFFER. *[2 Corinthians 1:6]*

"I will not allow myself to behave as a victim."

WE WERE UNDER GREAT PRESSURE, FAR BEYOND OUR ABILITY TO ENDURE, SO THAT WE DESPAIRED EVEN OF LIFE. INDEED, IN OUR HEARTS WE FELT THE SENTENCE OF DEATH. BUT THIS HAPPENED THAT WE MIGHT NOT RELY ON OURSELVES BUT ON GOD, WHO RAISES THE DEAD. *[2 Corinthians 1:8b–9]*

"I am determined to keep pushing ahead."

FORGETTING WHAT IS BEHIND AND *STRAINING TOWARD WHAT IS AHEAD*, I PRESS ON *TOWARD THE GOAL* TO WIN THE PRIZE FOR WHICH GOD HAS CALLED ME HEAVENWARD IN CHRIST JESUS. *[Philippians 3:13b–14]*

"I am willing to grow and change and learn new roles."

"AS I WAS WITH MOSES, SO I WILL BE WITH YOU..." *[Joshua 1:5]*

"I can face the challenges of life without denying their existence or giving up."

HE HAS DELIVERED US FROM SUCH A DEADLY PERIL, AND HE WILL DELIVER US. *ON HIM WE HAVE SET OUR HOPE* THAT HE WILL CONTINUE TO DELIVER US. *[2 Corinthians 1:10]*

CONSIDER IT PURE JOY, MY BROTHERS, WHENEVER YOU FACE TRIALS OF MANY KINDS, BECAUSE YOU KNOW THAT THE TESTING OF YOUR FAITH DEVELOPS PERSEVERANCE. *[James 1:2–3]*

"Hope is eager expectation of something God has promised that will certainly happen in the future."

"Hope is not blind optimism, it is realistic optimism."

"A person of hope does not just live for the possibilities of tomorrow but sees the possibilities of today, even when it's not going well."

"A person of hope can say an emphatic *no* to stagnation and an energetic *yes* to life. Hope is allowing God's Spirit to set us free and draw us forward."

Definitions of biblical hope from H. Norman Wright's "Chosen for Blessing"

WEEK
6
SMALL GROUP

ENGAGE

1. Have you ever known anyone who carries a relatively light burden and yet complains constantly about it? What does that communicate to you about their hope foundation?

2. **KEY** How have you been responding differently to setbacks over the past few weeks as a result of the hope experience?

GROUP EXERCISE

1. **KEY** Go around the room, each group member reading an attitude and the accompanying verse in the "Attitudes for Survival" list out loud until you have read them all.

2. Which of the verses seems particularly helpful to you right now?

3. **KEY** Now take time for each group member to rate themselves from 1 to 10 (10 being highest) on how much each attitude is currently a part of your life. Now share with the group: What attitude had your highest ranking? What attitude do you need the greatest growth?

4. Now try this experiment: Agree to read the attitudes and the verses in this week's notes out loud every day until next week's meeting. Read them daily with real feeling and emphasis! Then next week reflect on how this has impacted your outlook. You will experience blessing!

5. **KEY** Read 2 Corinthians 1:1–11. This is the most autobiographical and personally transparent of all of Paul's letters in the Bible. Here he is honest about the tough times he has experienced. What pressures do you suppose Paul was facing that would cause him to despair even of life? *[2 Corinthians 7:5–7 & 11:25–28, & Acts 19:23–41]*

6. What do you think Paul meant when he said he "despaired even of life"?

7. What benefits did Paul see from his sufferings?

8. How have you seen this to be true in your own life?

9. **KEY** Have some group members share part of their faith story in answer to the following questions: What have you learned from your own experiences — when your life seemed to fall apart and you did not know how to put it back together again? How were you able to trust in God's promise in a difficult situation and, as a result, build a stronger foundation of hope in Him? How has your experience brought others hope?

APPLY

"Hope is not something I generate myself. It happens as I focus on who God is, how He perceives me, and what He promises about the present and the future."

1. What situation are you facing now that seems hopeless to you? Are you are trying to generate your own hope? How can you turn this situation over to God this week?

2. How would it change the way you "think, feel and live" if you embraced the fact that God is right now working to redeem, renew and restore you even in the midst of your shattered hope?

3. **KEY** What steps will you take this week to ensure you have more biblically based hope?

GROUP PROJECT

KEY Make this the final week of your food drive project! How are you doing so far in meeting your group goals? Remember this is not just about bringing food to the poor; it's about bringing hope!

PRAYER AND PRAISE

KEY Look back at your specific prayer request at the end of the first small group lesson. As you have focused on who God is, how He perceives you, and His promises about the future, how has your request been answered? How can your group continue to pray for you?

BEFORE YOU LEAVE

Take a few minutes to talk about where and when you will meet next week, and who will be in charge of any meals or snacks.

WEEK 7

OUR ULTIMATE HOPE!

Therefore, prepare your minds for action; be self-controlled; set your hope fully on the grace to be given you when Jesus Christ is revealed. *[1 Peter 1:13]*

DAY

43

SUNDAY

by René Schlaepfer

My Ultimate Hope

> I SAW THE HOLY CITY, THE NEW JERUSALEM, COMING DOWN OUT OF HEAVEN FROM GOD, PREPARED AS A BRIDE BEAUTIFULLY DRESSED FOR HER HUSBAND. *[Revelation 21:2]*

Read Revelation 21:1–4

Joni Eareckson Tada, who was paralyzed in a diving accident as a teenager, talks about the day she got married:

> I felt awkward as my girlfriends strained to shift my paralyzed body into a cumbersome wedding gown. No amount of corseting gave me a perfect shape. Then, as I was wheeling into the church, I ran over the hem of my dress, leaving a greasy tire mark. My paralyzed hands couldn't hold the bouquet. And my wheelchair, though decorated, was still a big, clunky machine. I certainly didn't feel like the picture-perfect magazine bride. I inched my chair out to catch a glimpse of Ken in front. There he was, tall and stately in his formal attire. I saw him looking for me, craning his neck to look up the aisle. My face flushed, and I suddenly couldn't wait to be with him. I had seen my beloved. The love in Ken's face had washed away all my feelings of unworthiness. In his eyes, I was his pure and perfect bride... How easy it is for us to think that we're utterly unlovely — especially to someone as lovely as Christ. **But He loves us with the bright eyes of a Bridegroom's love** and cannot wait for the day we are united with Him forever.

The Bible speaks of our resurrection and reunion with Christ as a wedding feast! In today's passage, the wedding metaphor is expanded to include the day all of creation — heaven and earth — is reunited with God perfectly. That day is our ultimate hope! And that's what we'll focus on this week.

Even though we know we're loved and accepted just as we are, the wedding will bring about a transformation:

> No more struggle with sin.
> No more suffering. No more tears. No more loss.
> Reunion. Reward. Restoration.

This is the great hope, to which every other kind of Christian hope points! As Joni says, **"On that day I will dance!"**

What do I know about the Bible's promises of resurrection hope for me?

PRAYER

Lord, thank You for the promise of resurrection, and for the reunion and restoration and release that go along with that hope!

Get Ready, Boys!

by René Schlaepfer

THEREFORE, PREPARE YOUR MINDS FOR ACTION; BE SELF-CONTROLLED; SET YOUR HOPE FULLY ON THE GRACE TO BE GIVEN YOU WHEN JESUS CHRIST IS REVEALED. *[1 Peter 1:13]*

Read 1 Peter 1:13–25

While on an expedition to the Antarctic, explorer Sir Ernest Shackleton and his 27 men encountered nightmarish conditions. Temperatures were as low as 100 degrees below zero Fahrenheit. Their ship, the *Endurance*, was caught in pack ice for ten months. Shackleton had to leave most of his men on Elephant Island to go for help.

After sailing a lifeboat through a storm, Shackleton finally reached a whaling station. Three times he tried to rescue his crew, but bad weather turned him back. Finally, ten months after he had left them, he found a narrow channel through the ice. When he finally got to Elephant Island, he was amazed to find his men not only alive and well, but all prepared to get aboard his ship. Later Sir Ernest asked how they were ready to leave so promptly the day he arrived. They told him that every morning their leader rolled up his sleeping bag, saying, **"Get your things ready, boys, the boss may come today."** That action not only got them ready to leave; it also infused them with a daily dose of hope.

Speaking of Christ's return, Scripture says the same basic thing: "Get your things ready, boys, the boss may come today." The point is not to predict Christ's return; the point is to live as if we'll meet Jesus today! Look at 1 Peter 1:13–25, where the author is addressing Christians who were in the middle of a great persecution. He wisely points them toward their future hope *"when Jesus Christ is revealed."* He reminds them that this world, including all the glory and power of men, is temporary.

Where do you set your hope — on the temporary things of this world, or on the work of Jesus Christ?

How can a belief that Jesus will return to restore God's kingdom bring hope? Why does this seem to be less a part of our faith today?

PRAYER

Lord, help me live with daily anticipation of the fulfillment of Your promises!

DAY

45

TUESDAY

by Laurie Schlaepfer

More than a Metaphor

✹*Read 1 Corinthians 15:12–28*

My dad died last year.

I hate death. You'd think we human beings would be okay with death by now. After all, we're told "it's perfectly natural," the "circle of life." But I've become more convinced than ever of the *unnaturalness* of death. Death invaded God's good creation as an intruder, and we know in our hearts we were never meant for it.

Since my dad's death, the resurrection of Christ has become more personally significant to me than ever before. I have believed in His resurrection since I was a child. But now in my grief I see it as a beacon of hope on a dark night.

It's a sad fact that many churches today have done away with belief in Christ's physical resurrection, instead making it mere metaphor. One pastor said, "the story is symbolic of the undying spirit of humanity." Another suggested, "The resurrection myth teaches merely that we can be 'resurrected' again and again in our lives."

Apparently some folks in the church in Corinth were also denying the possibility of physical resurrection. Paul writes to firmly remind them that the physical resurrection of Jesus is at the core of the gospel message that he and all the apostles had preached from day one. **And the resurrection is at the core of our hope.** On that first Easter Sunday morning, life invaded death and conquered it. Jesus' resurrection is the guarantee for the future resurrection of all who belong to Him. And more: It is a peek at the renewal of all creation, heaven and earth.

If there was no physical resurrection, then as Paul puts it, "your faith is futile," literally a waste of time. If our hope in Christ is only for this life, what kind of "hope" is that?

But Christ indeed was raised! And when He returns, those who are in Him will be raised as well. That includes my dad.

It's by looking back at the resurrection of Christ that I can look to the future with outrageous hope. I'll see my dad again — more alive, more *physical*, that he ever was. *"Death has been swallowed up in victory. Where, O death, is your victory? Where, O death, is your sting?"*

Am I placing my confident hope in the resurrection and re-creation the Bible promises? If you have doubts, try an experiment this week: Try living as if you believed the Bible's resurrection promises and see what happens!

PRAYER

Lord, thank You for the promise of resurrection and renewal, not just metaphorically, but literally! I believe... help my unbelief!

Future Certain Hope

by Gary Williams

...PUTTING ON... THE HOPE OF SALVATION AS A HELMET...
[1 Thessalonians 5:8]

✹ *Read 1 Thessalonians 5:1–11*

Now here's something that sounds like an oxymoron: *"certain hope."* How certain can hope be? The Greek word *elpis* means to *"anticipate with pleasure and to expect with confidence."* Yes! We can look forward to it and it *will* happen! Salvation *will* happen! Christians *will* ultimately escape the hardships of this world. We *will* enter Heaven with God — the culmination of our salvation experience.

How interesting that this "hope of salvation" is reflected as a "helmet"; a head protector. Could this reflect the importance of having a *mindset*, set on Jesus, the author and perfecter of our faith? *[Hebrews 12:2]*

Hope is a protector. Hope is faith holding out its hand in the dark. It is, *"Christ in you, the hope of glory" [Colossians 1:27]*. It previews that *"blessed hope — the glorious appearing of our great God and Savior, Jesus Christ." [Titus 2:13]*

Without hope life is meaningless — meaning less and less. I stood before a dying man who had no future hope. With less than an hour to live he was too weak to speak or open his eyes. Time was short so I had him squeeze my hand once for "yes" and twice for "no." After carefully presenting the salvation plan of Jesus, I asked if he wanted to become a believer. He squeezed my hand once, so we prayed the prayer. When asked if he really understood, a huge smile filled his face. This father died 20 minutes later.

His son, overwhelmed with joy, exclaimed, "My miserable father has not smiled for five years. Now I know he died with hope in his heart!"

"Hope springs eternal in the human breast." *Mother Teresa*

1 Thessalonians 5:1–11 says we're living in the light, not darkness. In what ways do I darken my thoughts by questioning my future hope of salvation and how can I add light to that mindset?

PRAYER

Lord, help me set my mind on the hope of complete salvation, the day not just my soul, but all of me, will be saved from sin and death.

DAY

47

THURSDAY

by Meg Imel

Endurance Inspired by Hope

WE CONTINUALLY REMEMBER BEFORE OUR GOD AND FATHER YOUR WORK PRODUCED BY FAITH, YOUR LABOR PROMPTED BY LOVE, AND YOUR ENDURANCE INSPIRED BY HOPE IN OUR LORD JESUS CHRIST. *[1 Thessalonians 1:3]*

✹ ***Read 1 Thessalonians 1:2–3***

When I became a Christian at 34, my brother-in-law said, "Meg, if God can save you, He can save anyone!" Now, I'm not sure if he was referring to my not-so-lily-white past or my stubborn, hard heart.

I admit I am a Type A "lion" and also a bit of a stubborn pessimist. So 1 Thessalonians 1:3 is a challenge for me. I understand *"work produced by faith,"* and *"labor prompted by love."* But, do I have endurance inspired by hope? Hope for what I cannot now experience? That's what Romans 8:24–25 says I am to have:

FOR IN THIS HOPE WE WERE SAVED. BUT HOPE THAT IS SEEN IS NO HOPE AT ALL. WHO HOPES FOR WHAT HE ALREADY HAS? BUT IF WE HOPE FOR WHAT WE DO NOT YET HAVE, WE WAIT FOR IT PATIENTLY.

Do I live in hope for His return? Do I fix my eyes beyond the realities of this life?

I know when the doctors told us our oldest son had a rare cancer in the lymph system of the skin, I was afraid. It took us months to find out that the disease was treatable and not life threatening, but not before I wrestled with God. When I finally acknowledged that Ryan was God's child first, that God loved him more than I could, and that I was thankful for Ryan no matter what happened, I could find hope. A hope where I could believe that something good would happen, no matter what. What peace we have knowing that believers will be united in heaven! It should be the only motivation I need to live my life for God alone.

Where is your hope?

In what ways is endurance inspired by hope? How do I see this truth at work in the worlds of sports or business? What lessons can I draw spiritually?

PRAYER

Lord, thank You for saving me. Help me to live today with the hope of Christ's return clearly in my mind and heart.

Does Hope Make a Difference?

DAY

48

FRIDAY

by René Schlaepfer

BROTHERS, WE DO NOT WANT YOU TO BE IGNORANT ABOUT THOSE WHO FALL ASLEEP, OR TO GRIEVE LIKE THE REST OF MEN, WHO HAVE NO HOPE. *[1 Thessalonians 4:13]*

Read 1 Thessalonians 4:13–18

I had just finished speaking at the funeral of a young woman when one of her male friends strode up to me and, in front of the other mourners, said, "That's all B.S.! Everything you said about heaven and Jesus — all B.S.! Whether you believe or not, it all ends the same, doesn't it? Doesn't it?!"

I waited until he had blown off a little more steam, and then asked, "Do you really want an answer?" He was surprised, but nodded yes.

"Then," I said, "Come with me right now, because I'm going directly from this funeral service to visit two people in the cancer wing at the hospital. One is the father of a friend. He never made room for God, and is now an old man petrified of dying. He's literally white-knuckling his ride into eternity, gripping the side rails of his bed, staring ahead with panicked eyes. I try to speak words of comfort, but I don't know if he even hears me.

"After that, walk with me down the hall to see my friend Meryl. She's dying, too, in the last stages of cancer. But when you enter her room it's like you've walked into some kind of a special serenity zone, peace perfuming the place like incense. **She radiates calm confidence as she welcomes her visitors and speaks of soon seeing her Savior.** Then — only after you have seen the difference between them — only then, tell me that it's all B.S."

He walked away, nervously refusing to go on a visit that I think might have changed his life forever. But if you ever wonder why pastors still believe after they've seen so much death as part of their calling, you need to know: **We have seen the difference that Christian hope makes.**

Again, read 1 Thessalonians 4:13–18. The apostle Paul is talking about the great hope, the promise of the return of Christ and all it includes. When someone you know is down, encourage them with these words!

How can I encourage myself and others today with the hope Paul speaks of in these verses?

PRAYER

Lord, thank You for the promise that, ultimately, You have my destiny and the destiny of the world in Your hands!

DAY

49

SATURDAY

by René Schlaepfer

Hope Review

In many ways, this hope study has been an attempt to recover authentic Christian hope, the kind of hope that motivated the earliest Christians to endure suffering and show compassion:

- The hope inspired by Jesus Christ's resurrection from the dead, which can comfort me personally with the promise that I will rise — but can also comfort me about the future of all of creation, since the Bible sees Christ's resurrection as a sure sign that God will bring His kingdom to earth
- The hope that follows from the conviction that ultimately God is in control of history
- The hope that grows from the promise that not even one cup of water, or any other good deed done in the name of Christ, will go unrewarded
- The hope that comes from knowing that absolutely everything that happens to me, even suffering, will be used by God to grow me and others into Christ-like character

That is unshakable hope!

We started seven weeks ago by posing four questions:

What is my view of God?

Christian hope says God loves me and plans the best for me.

> Find rest, O my soul, in God alone; *my hope comes from him.* He alone is my rock and my salvation; he is my fortress, I will not be shaken. *[Psalm 62:5–6]*

What is my view of myself?

Christian hope says I have God's unlimited power in me for whatever lies ahead.

> I pray that your hearts will be flooded with light so that you can understand the *confident hope* he has given to those he called — his holy people who are his rich and glorious inheritance. I also pray that you will

understand the incredible greatness of God's power for us who believe him. This is the same mighty power that raised Christ from the dead... *[Ephesians 1:18–20a NLT]*

What will the future bring?

Christian hope says I have an unshakable inheritance! Plus God has a plan for me for good, and not for evil.

"For I know the plans I have for you," declares the Lord, "plans to prosper you and not to harm you, *plans to give you a hope and a future.*" *[Jeremiah 29:11]*

What is the outcome of suffering?

Christian hope says God will use every hard time in my life for His perfect plan, and the outcome of suffering will be Christ-likeness.

And we know that *in all things God works for the good of those who love him*, who have been called according to his purpose. *[Romans 8:28]*

Here's my hope for you and me — the verse that started this whole experience seven weeks ago:

May the God of hope fill you with all joy and peace as you trust in him, so that you may *overflow with hope* by the power of the Holy Spirit. *[Romans 15:13]*

How have I seen this emphasis on Christian hope make a difference in my life?

PRAYER

Lord, thank You for all my reasons for hope. May I be a Christ-follower overflowing with hope to those all around me!

ACTION

Spread Hope Project: Have a celebration service with your small group and church. Share personal stories about how you have grown in hope, and how you have spread hope to others. Invite a friend to the celebration service so they can personally see and experience a roomful of believers in Jesus inspired by hope!

DAY

50

SUNDAY

by René Schlaepfer

Celebrate Hope!

THEN ALL THE PEOPLE WENT AWAY TO EAT AND DRINK, TO SEND PORTIONS OF FOOD AND TO *CELEBRATE WITH GREAT JOY*, BECAUSE THEY NOW UNDERSTOOD THE WORDS THAT HAD BEEN MADE KNOWN TO THEM. *[Nehemiah 8:12]*

Total hopelessness. That's how the book of Nehemiah starts. All of Israel is in deep gloom over the future of the nation. Their cities are utterly destroyed, their Scriptures have been forgotten, the walls of Jerusalem lie in ruins, and their morale has hit absolute rock-bottom. They're convinced there is nothing good ahead for them.

Then Nehemiah shows up. He says God has sent him to help them rebuild both the physical walls and the spiritual walls of their nation. With a burst of enthusiasm, and despite fierce opposition, all of the men, women and children get to work. And within just 52 days, the ruined wall of Jerusalem is rebuilt. In fact, the people use the rubble of the ruins to fortify and thicken the new wall, so that it is higher and wider than ever before.

More importantly, the people rediscover the Scriptures. Their priests explain to them the meaning of their Bible. They gain a new sense of destiny. **In just 52 days, after years of neglect, their situation completely changes from hopeless to hope-filled!**

Then Nehemiah tells them to celebrate what has happened to them. And as you read in today's verse, after 52 days of hard work, they spend some time in serious celebration!

Well, we have just spent approximately the same amount of time doing something very similar: Rebuilding the walls of our lives. Remembering Scripture that was, perhaps, forgotten: Rediscovering that God has a future hope for us! And now it is time to celebrate! If you can, follow the Israelite example and have a dinner party. Share with others, perhaps in your small group, what God has done in your life.

And remember, God transforms our lives by changing what we think. This book has been an attempt to compare what the world tells you with what God tells you. **Which one you choose to believe — every day — will make all the difference between having genuine hope and feeling hopeless.** Now that you have started, continue your new, hopeful way of thinking!

In what ways have you been changed for the better during this study? What can you do to continue those good changes?

PRAYER

Lord, thank You for Your hope! Help me to continue to grow in hope and to spread hope to those around me.

Small Group Lesson 7

WEEK
7
SMALL GROUP

The Ultimate Hope

LEADER'S NOTE Please review these questions before beginning in order to select those that will be most meaningful and effective for your group. Do not feel obligated to answer them all. But please try to discuss at least one from each section, especially the **KEY** questions, allowing adequate time for prayer and to discuss the group assignment.

CONNECT

1. **KEY** What caught your attention, challenged or encouraged you in the weekend message or the devotionals?

2. Have you ever thought, "Man, if this happens, I'm going to die!" Maybe it was something serious or just an amusement park ride or turbulent airplane experience. What thoughts and emotions were swirling in your head at that moment?

3. **KEY** Break into two groups. In 60 seconds, have each group list as many movies, TV shows, songs, and books about the afterlife as they possibly can. The group that wins this competition gets an all-expense paid trip to Fresno, California! Just kidding (insert your Fresno-related joke about the afterlife here). Have a member of each group jot their group's answers in the margin to the right… ready, set, go!

   Which group listed more?

   Now, looking at both lists, what sorts of unbiblical ideas about the afterlife did these movies, books, songs, or TV shows promote?

   - ❑ We float around on clouds
   - ❑ It's just like life on earth, but with superpowers
   - ❑ We keep coming back to earth as different people
   - ❑ We come back as ghosts — and we don't know we're dead!!
   - ❑ Other ideas:______________________________________

WEEK 7

SMALL GROUP

WATCH THE VIDEO

This is a crucial part of Christian hope: What happens after death!

Here's what you can look forward to, according to the Bible, if you have given your life to Christ:

1. ______________________________ of Christ

2. ______________________________

3. ______________________________ of heaven and earth

4. ______________________________

5. ______________________________

> May the God of hope fill you with all joy and peace as you trust in him, so that you may overflow with hope by the power of the Holy Spirit. *[Romans 15:13]*

ENGAGE

1. Who was the first family member you recall dying? What effect did their death have on you?

2. Which future event (return of Christ, resurrection, re-creation of heaven and earth, reunion, or reward) do you look forward to the most, and why?

3. Which of those five future events do you think is least known — or least believed — by Christians today? Why? What negative impact does this lack of understanding about the Bible's teaching have on Christians?

4. **KEY** Read 1 Thessalonians 4:13–18. What do you think Paul means when he says he does not want the Christians "to grieve like the rest of men, who have no hope"?

5. How do Paul's words here bring hope even to grieving people?

6. **KEY** Read Revelation 21:1–4. What is it about this description of the new heaven and the new earth that especially appeals to you? Why?

6. **KEY** Read 1 Corinthians 15:12–20. Reading between the lines of this Scripture, what were some critics apparently saying about the resurrection?

7. **KEY** How did the Apostle Paul respond to this accusation? Does his response surprise you in any way?

8. What new insight does this verse reveal to you?

9. Why do you think the foundation of Christian hope is the resurrection of Christ and His return?

10. How could last week have been different if you truly lived each moment in light of these promises? What actions would you have taken, or not taken? What attitudes would you have had or not had?

APPLY

1. **KEY** In what area of your life do you sense God calling you to turn to Him and live in light of this ultimate hope?

2. What steps can you take this week to achieve this?

3. How will this change your attitude and actions tomorrow?

PRAYER AND PRAISE

KEY Take time as a group to reflect on what the Holy Spirit is revealing to you as a result of this hope experience and praise God for how your hope has grown:

Share with the group how they can continue to pray for you.

BEFORE YOU LEAVE

Take some pictures of your group tonight and post them online at: www.HopeExperience.com

Talk about posting your group's story at www.HopeExperience.com. Include information like: How have lives been changed? How did your group project go?

Who will be in charge of writing and sending the email?

Talk about your future as a small group. Where will you go from here? Will you continue to meet? When and where? What will you study? (You can visit **www.tlc.org/smallgroups** for ideas)

SMALL GROUP RESOURCES

Small Group Guidelines and Agreement

It's a good idea for every group to put words to their shared values, expectations, and commitments. Such guidelines will help you avoid unspoken agendas and unmet expectations. We recommend you discuss your guidelines during your first meeting in order to lay the foundation for a healthy group experience. Feel free to add anything that is important to your group.

✹ We agree to the following values:

CLEAR PURPOSE To grow healthy, spiritual lives by building a healthy Small Group community.

GROUP ATTENDANCE To give priority to the group meeting (call if I am absent or late).

SAFE ENVIRONMENT To create a safe place where people can be heard and feel loved (no quick answers, snap judgments, or simple fixes).

BE CONFIDENTIAL To keep anything that is shared strictly confidential and within the group.

CONFLICT RESOLUTION To avoid gossip and to immediately resolve any concerns by following the principles of Matthew 18:15–17 which begins with going directly to the person with whom you have an issue.

SPIRITUAL HEALTH To give group members permission to help me live a healthy, balanced spiritual life that is pleasing to God.

LIMIT OUR FREEDOM To limit our freedom by not serving or consuming alcohol during Small Group meetings or events so as to avoid causing a weaker brother or sister to stumble. *[1 Corinthians 8:1–13, Romans 14:19–21]*

WELCOME NEWCOMERS To invite our friends who might benefit from this study and warmly welcome newcomers

BUILDING RELATIONSHIPS To get to know the other members of the group and pray for them regularly.

OTHER

We agree to the following items:

- Refreshments/Mealtimes ______________________________
- Childcare ______________________________
- When we will meet (day of week) ______________________________
- Where we will meet (place) ______________________________
- The time we'll meet at is ______________________________
- The time we'll end by is ______________________________
- Review date of this agreement ______________________________

Small Group Values

WE WANT OUR SMALL GROUPS TO BE...

- **Authentic**

  We live in a world where people don't have to interact with one another. We can go for years without even talking to our neighbors. The church needs to be a place where people can know one another and be known, and Small Groups are communities made up of 6–10 people in which this is possible. Small Groups are a safe place to share and do life together. Our desire is that Small Groups be all about learning together, growing together, laughing together, crying together and eating together all with the goal of becoming more like Jesus together.

- **Organic**

  It is our desire at Twin Lakes Church that a portion of your Small Group be formed in an organic and dynamic way. One way people are going to join a Small Group is through invitation. This means that the leader needs to be out in the greater Twin Lakes Church community meeting people and inviting them to their Small Group. Invitations can also happen through group members inviting others to join. People will also join through a connection event and through inquiring about open groups at TLC.

- **Bibliocentric**

  The Word of God is necessary for knowing God and growing in the Christian life. One main aspect of our Small Groups will be the study and application of the Bible.

- **Missional**

  Our Small Groups will not only meet together to study and share life, they will also commit to serving our community. We will do this through ShareFest, the food drive, Spread Hope projects, and writing encouragement notes. But don't limit yourselves — be creative!

Guidelines for a Great Group

- **Be consistent**

  It is expected that Small Group members will be present every week. Consistency helps people in the group to get to know each other and trust each other.

- **Be prepared**

  The Hope series consists of three parts: daily devotionals, weekly sermons and weekly small groups. It's important to keep current with all three. If you miss a sermon, please catch it online. If you miss a devotional, please double up the next day.

- **Be real**

  Small Groups aren't a place for people to come and act like they have it all together. Nobody does except for God Himself. Small Groups should be a safe place for people to be real with their struggles, sin, hurts and joys. If this kind of sharing isn't happening in your Small Group, be the first to share honestly; others will follow your example!

- **Be together**

  Enjoy each other's company. Share a dessert before or after your Small Group meeting. Spend time with one another outside of weekly meetings. It is important for the leader to set the stage for community. ShareFest is a great way — plan a project you can participate in together as a group.

- **Be curious**

  Ask each other questions and share with one another what your lives are all about. Share testimonies. Share "highs and lows." Regularly get into each other's lives through questions like: "What is your story?" "Where have you come from in life?" "What issues impact your faith?" "What are your hopes and dreams?" "What's one thing you are passionately praying about?

- **Be responsible**

  Be responsible with personal information shared in your Small Group. Love and encourage each other, but please don't gossip.

Small Group Roster

NAME	EMAIL	PHONE

Small Group Prayer Requests

Questions Asked Frequently by Hosts

- **Can I get a friend to help me host?**

  Absolutely! We encourage you to pair up with another friend or couple. Together you can share the role of host and pray for the people God brings to your group.

- **Do I need to be a "Bible expert" to host?**

  Nope! The most important things that you need are a desire to serve the members of your group and to grow in your own personal relationship with Christ. We will provide you with training and easy-to-use curriculum.

- **How many people should I be expecting to accommodate?**

  An optimum number of people to have in a Small Group is 8–10, but larger and smaller groups can work too. A larger group can always split into "sub-groups" for discussion and prayer.

- **What is my commitment?**

  As a host, we are asking that you open your home for about 90 minutes a week for the 7 weeks of this study. We ask that at each meeting you show the teaching DVD, go through the curriculum and pray together as a group.

- **How do I get people to come be part of my Small Group?**

  We will have a time at church when people can sign up for a Small Group near their home. You are also encouraged to invite people you know to your Small Group.

We are interested in impacting people for eternity, whoever they are. You will be a significant part of this campaign that will spiritually transform this community! If you have questions email us at smallgroups@tlc.org

20 Ideas for Spreading Hope

"And if you give even a cup of cold water to one of the least of my followers, you will surely be rewarded."
[Matthew 10:42 NLT]

1. Participate in a church-organized community service project.
2. Buy someone a soft drink or coffee and have an encouraging conversation.
3. Read a hope-building book to a child (e.g., *You Are Special* by Max Lucado).
4. Write a note of thanks to a family member.
5. Tell a friend or family member where you see them as skilled or talented.
6. Visit an elderly person or shut-in (alone or with a church group).
7. Give to the needy: food, clothes, time.
8. Make a meal for someone who is sick; include a hope-building note.
9. Write a note to someone who seems down; include hopeful verses.
10. Bless someone with your spoken words today.
11. Give to someone anonymously.
12. Bring enough lunch to share with a co-worker.
13. Write a note of thanks to someone at your church; perhaps an unsung hero or key volunteer.
14. Rake or mow a neighbor's yard.
15. Visit someone in prison or jail. They need hope!
16. Write to someone in the military. Your church has names and addresses.
17. Thank the person who led you to Christ, or a person who discipled you.
18. Bring cookies or flowers to a neighbor.
19. Babysit for a mother who could use a break.
20. Say one kind thing to each checker or salesperson you encounter today.

Songs About Hope

Interested in making a playlist of songs that inspire you to have hope — and bring hope to others? Here's a list of suggestions to get you started. Be forewarned: This reflects my own extremely eclectic musical tastes, so there are all sorts of genres represented here, from country to rock to R&B!

Most of these are by Christian artists, but at the end I added a few songs I found uplifting by secular artists too. We'll post this online at www.HopeExperience.com so you can add your own suggestions!

"Hope Now" by Addison Road

"My Hope" & "Mighty to Save" by Hillsong

"Only Hope" by Caedmon's Call

"There Will Be A Day" by Jeremy Camp

"I Will Rise" Chris Tomlin

"Our Hope Endures" by Natalie Grant

> Sometimes the sun stays hidden for years
> Sometimes the sky rains night after night, when will it clear?
> But our hope endures the worst of conditions
> It's more than our optimism:
> Let the earth quake, our hope is unchanged!

"Hold Onto Jesus" by Steven Curtis Chapman

"A New Song" by Matt Brouwer

> We wait in hope for the Lord, He is our help and our shield
> We wait in hope for the Lord, He is our help in the darkest hour
> To my fear I will not be held captive anymore

"You Are My Stronghold" by Watermark

"If I Stand" & *"My Deliverer"* by Rich Mullins

"With Hope" by Steven Curtis Chapman

> We can cry with hope, we can say goodbye with hope,
> 'Cause we know our goodbye is not the end.
> And we can grieve with hope, 'cause we believe with hope!

"My Life Is In Your Hands" by Kirk Franklin and God's Property

"You Don't Know" by Kierra Kiki Sheard

"It Might Be Hope" & *"He's Always Been Faithful"* Sara Groves

> I can't remember a trial or a pain
> He did not recycle to bring me gain.
> I can't remember one single regret in serving God
> Only and trusting His hand.
> All I have need of His hand will provide.
> He's always been faithful to me.

HOPE RESOURCES

"Hope For Tomorrow" by Mike Rimmey

"He Knows My Name" by Tommy Walker

"You Are" by The Katinas

> I'm hurting Lord, this world can hit me so hard.
> Heal me with Your grace... You are my strength at all times.
> There is nothing I will fear 'cause You are here.
> You are my refuge and hope.

"Go Light Your World" various artists, inc. Chris Rice and Kathy Troccoli

"Be Lifted or Hope Rising" by The David Crowder Band

"In Christ Alone (My Hope Is Found)" various artists, including Keith and Krystyn Getty, Newsboys, etc.

"You Are My Hope" by Skillet

> Times are hard, times have changed, don't you say?
> But I keep holding on to You.
> It's hard to keep the faith alive day to day,
> Leaning on the strength I've found in You.
> You're the hope of all the earth.

"On Eagles Wings", "You Are Loved, Don't Give Up" & *"You Raise Me Up"* by Josh Groban

"Song of Hope" by Robbie Seay Band

> I will sing a song of hope. Sing along!
> God of heaven come down, Heaven come down.

"Only Hope" by Mandy Moore

"Hope" by Fat Freddy's Drop

"Beautiful Day" by U2

"Hope of Deliverance" by Paul McCartney

"Here Comes The Sun" by The Beatles

"Hold On" by Wilson Phillips

"Wait And See (He's Not Finished With Me Yet)" Brandon Heath

> There is hope, for me yet, because God won't forget
> All the plans He's made for me.
> I have to wait and see, He's not finished with me yet,
> He's not finished with me yet.

IT MIGHT BE HOPE

You do your work the best that you can
You put one foot in front of the other
Life comes in waves and makes it's demands
You hold on as well as you're able

You've been here for a long long time
Hope has a way of turning it's face to you
Just when you least expect it
You walk in a room
You look out a window
And something there leaves you breathless
You say to yourself it's been a while
since I felt this
But it feels like it might be hope

It's hard to recall what blew out the flame
It's been dark since you can remember
You talk it all through to find it a name
As days go on by without number

You've been here for a long long time
Hope has a way of turning it's face to you
Just when you least expect it
You walk in a room
You look out a window
And something there leaves you breathless
You say to yourself it's been a while
since I felt this
But it feels like it might be hope

— Sara Groves

Here are more books devoted to a study of biblical hope. Some are for specific situations, such as divorce or death, while others are more general Bible studies.

For Further Study

Hope For the Separated: Wounded Marriages Can Be Healed
by Gary Chapman

The One Year Book of Hope
by Nancy Guthrie

Holding On to Hope: A Pathway through Suffering to the Heart of God
by Nancy Guthrie

Hope Beyond Reason: Embraced by God's Presence in the Toughest of Times
by Dave Hess

Hope for Hurting Hearts
by Greg Laurie

Surprised by Hope: Rethinking Heaven, the Resurrection, and the Mission of the Church
by N. T. Wright

Walking with the God Who Cares: Finding Hope When You Need It Most
by Catherine Martin

Living a Life of Hope
by Nathan Busenitz

Hope: The Best of Things
by Joni Eareckson Tada

Meet the Authors

CHARLIE BROXTON Charlie is the pastor of our Genesis ministries. He and his wife Nancy have two children.

DAN BAKER Former program director at Camp Hammer, Dan has been the worship pastor at TLC for seventeen years.

DAVE HICKS Legendary youth pastor for many years at Oakland Covenant Church and then senior pastor in Southern California, Dave is now our Pastor of Adult Ministries at TLC.

GARY WILLIAMS For many years the beloved Children's Pastor at TLC, Gary currently directs the extensive Pastoral Care and Second Half Adult ministries at TLC.

HANNAH DEUTSCH A former Camp Hammer and TLC staff member, Hannah is currently very busy in her role as mother of three and leader in the MOPS ministry. She and her husband, Kevin, are active in reaching out to young people and encouraging them in their faith.

JIM JOSSELYN Pastor of Community Life Ministries at TLC, Jim and his wife Suzi have three great kids.

KELLY WELTY Multimedia director at TLC, Kelly is responsible for all of the on-screen media you see, plus the lighting for each service. He and his wife Laurie have two children.

KEVIN DEUTSCH Husband to Hannah and father of three, Kevin is a graphic designer at TLC. He is active in many areas of service, primarily discipleship.

KIM BREUNINGER Director of Women's Ministries at TLC for many years now, Kim is married to Dave Breuninger, director of Koinonia Conference Center.

LAURIE SCHLAEPFER The better half of René, Laurie is a student of world religions, focusing in particular on Islam and Mormonism. In addition to her roles as wife and mother, Laurie also teaches world religion courses at Western Seminary.

MARK HILLENGA Pastor of Life Development Ministries at TLC, Mark directs a large staff in their care of hundreds of children and students each week, from infants to college.

MARK SPURLOCK Director of Camp Hammer for many years, Mark is now Executive Pastor at Twin Lakes Church. He and his wife Lora have three children.

MEG IMEL Meg serves as the principal at Twin Lakes Christian School. She has an extensive background in education having served for years at Baymonte Christian School. Meg and her husband Jerry have three children.

PAUL SPURLOCK Pastor of Outreach at TLC, Paul has also been our youth pastor and on staff at Camp Hammer.

RENÉ SCHLAEPFER René has been senior pastor of Twin Lakes Church for 16 years. He and his wife Laurie have three great kids!

ROBIN SPURLOCK Former director of Ponderosa Conference Center, Robin is married to Pastor Paul Spurlock and serves as an administrative assistant at TLC.

VALERIE WEBB TLC Office Manager and administrative assistant to René and Mark, Valerie has served in a bewildering array of jobs both at TLC and Camp Hammer for many years.